I Was
An
Appraiser/Assessor

Contents

Preface

I didn't set out to become an appraiser. Like most little kids, I went through several career wishes including veterinarian, preacher, and FBI agent before settling on the law. The latter became my focus entering undergraduate training and I even went on to a challenging three semesters in law school before deciding to seek other alternatives. An advisor told me law school requires a unique way of thinking that not everyone can achieve. My failure to accomplish that way of thinking is my excuse for leaving and I'm sticking to it.

The local county attorney, who helped me get into law school, also helped me get a job after I left law school. The job involved counseling juvenile delinquents in a newly created facility that took them out of the local jail. It was rewarding psychologically to help young men see the error of their ways, which is good since it was not financially rewarding.

Fortunately, another job opened with a local social service agency as a grant writer and program planner. The agency actually received credit for raising a family out of poverty just by hiring me, which was also rewarding in its own way. However, living just above the prevailing poverty level did not appeal to me in the long run.

Fortunately, one of the board members of this social service agency was a county commissioner and he encouraged me to apply for the position of county appraiser when that position became vacant. The position offered a significant pay hike, the offices were in my town and it offered a retirement program not offered by the social service agency. So, I took it with the intent of staying long enough to find something better; and after 40+ years I did – retirement.

The peculiar thing is most of my colleagues in the mass appraisal/assessment profession came to the profession in a similar fashion. Very few people know anything about mass appraisal, much less little kids looking to their future. Instead, they fall into it after doing something else for a while, and then they decide to stay. They may stay for the stability of working for local government, or because the job is close to home or a myriad of other reasons. The better ones stay for the challenges.

I have been very blessed to have practiced my new profession working in three local jurisdictions in Kansas then moving to the International Association of Assessing Officers (IAAO), where I was able to teach and write and consult with assessors all over the world. By and large, the people I worked with were hard working, honest people who just wanted to do a good job. Most did and this book is dedicated to them. However, it is my sincere hope that members of the general public will read this book to gain a little insight into the job of the local assessor/appraiser and hopefully some appreciation for the difficulty of doing it right.

Dedication

A life, a book is not developed without help along the way. I am truly grateful for all the teachers and mentors who helped me evolve into the appraiser I became. There are too many to name individually and their names would likely mean little outside the mass appraisal profession, where many are considered giants.

Most of all I want to thank my wife, Mary, who stood by me and encouraged me all the way. She has been a shoulder to lean on as well as a sounding board who forced me to cut through the jargon. She made me a teacher who could take complex terms and explain them so "even she" could understand them. The result was an even deeper understanding on my part. If you read this book and understand what it says, thank her.

Our Tax System

In order to understand and appreciate what your local assessor does, it helps to know how the tax system works in the United States.

Our tax system is based on taxing the wealth held by taxpayers. That wealth is represented in three ways: how much a person earns (income tax), how much that person buys (sales tax), and the value of property that person owns (property tax). This idea is represented in taxation text books as the "three-legged stool". The only way a three-legged  stool stays balanced is when all three legs are present and are used properly. Our tax system is in balance only when income, sales and property taxes are present and used properly. A person may not have a job where they earn taxable income. That same person still has to buy food that is subject to the sales tax. He or she might own property that is subject to the property tax. In the same way, an individual who rents a house or apartment still buys food and may earn a taxable income. Our tax system is built to use all three taxes in a way that doesn't create a hardship for anyone.

At least that's the theory. Unfortunately, local counties, cities, and school districts have to rely on money the property tax brings in. That is because the law doesn't allow them to use any money brought in by the income tax and very little from the sales tax. For example, in many states the county has to manage the property tax system. That means it collects all property taxes and distributes them to cities, school districts and other taxing districts within the county. That also means the county has to answer the questions and complaints regarding that tax, even though the amount actually spent by the county is a small percentage of the total tax. The county will be used as the local property tax administrative agency throughout this book.

One of the county's responsibilities is to estimate the value of property to be taxed. That is the where the assessor comes into play. The amount of the income tax is based on the taxpayer's income. The amount of sales tax is based on the selling price of an item bought by the taxpayer. The amount of property tax to be paid is based on the value of the taxpayer's property. Taxpayers fill out income tax forms every year and pay the amount they calculate as being owed to the government. Sales taxes are collected by the store where the taxpayer shops. The county assessor estimates the value of the taxpayer's property. That value then forms one half of the property tax formula. The other half is the multiplier that will meet the budgetary needs for the cities and school districts within the county.

Cycles

State law tells the county when property tax statements are to be mailed to all property owners each year. Several things have to happen before that is done.

1. The assessor must estimate a value for all properties in the county.
2. The County Clerk sends those values to cities, school districts and special districts.
3. They use that information to calculate their budgets.
4. Those budgets are sent back to the County Clerk.

5. The County Clerk calculates the tax bills based on the property value and the amount of the budget needed.
6. Those tax bills are sent to the Treasurer or Collector to be mailed to the property owners.

Every step in this cycle is prescribed by state law that dictates who is to do what, when and in some cases how. Taxpayers think of this as an annual cycle, but steps within it may involve more than one calendar year. For example, the assessor may do the work of estimating values in one year. Property owners have a right to appeal those values. Then the final values are used for property tax purposes the following year.

We will use five properties to illustrate the taxing process. Three of the properties are residential. Two are commercial properties. All of them are located in a city that has a budget of $100,000. The table below shows the process. The five properties are identified as 1 through 5. Their market values are shown in the second column. The mill rate or tax rate for the city is shown in the third column. The taxes that each property is charged is shown in the far-right column.

Market value is the amount of money an owner can expect to be paid for a piece of property. A more formal definition is:

A value, stated as an opinion, that presumes the transfer of a property (i.e., a right of ownership or a bundle of such rights), as of a certain date, under specific conditions set forth in the value definition that is identified by the appraiser as applicable in an appraisal.

Property	Market Value	Mill Rate	Taxes
1	250,000	0.04347826	$10,869.57
2	125,000	0.04347826	$5,434.78
3	450,000	0.04347826	$19,565.22
4	875,000	0.04347826	$38,043.48
5	600,000	0.04347826	$26,086.96
Totals	2,300,000		$100,000.01

Taxes are calculated by multiplying the market value by the mill rate. That is possible when the assessor estimates a single dollar amount for each property. Market value, on the other hand, is best represented as a range of possibilities. The size of that range depends on things. The buyer may be a better negotiator than the seller. The weather may have been exceptionally bad or good on the day the property was shown. The reason for an appraisal may determine where an appraisal falls. For example, a bank is only interested in getting back the amount it loans to the buyer. It will settle for an appraisal equal to that amount, even though the property may sell for more. On the other hand, a person selling their house will want to know the maximum amount that house will bring. Most assessors try to estimate a value toward the middle of that range in order to consider both extremes.

Assume the assessor has appraised a house for $250,000. Houses like that are selling for prices from $225,000 to $275,000. A bank that loans money for that house may require a down payment of 10% of the total sale price. The down payment would be $25,000 with a selling price of $250,000. That leaves $225,000 that the bank will loan on that house. The bank hires an appraiser to determine whether the house is worth at least the $225,000 loan amount. On the other hand, the owner may look for an appraiser who will estimate a price closer to $275,000.

State agencies measure the assessor's results by dividing the assessor's value by the actual selling price of the property.

Assessor's Value	$250,000
Actual Selling Price	÷250,000
Ratio	1.00

The assessor has done an acceptable job when that ratio is between 0.90 and 1.10.

	Examples			
	1	2	3	4
Assessor's Value	250,000	250,000	225,000	275,000
Actual Selling Price	225,000	275,000	275,000	225,000
Ratios	1.10	0.90	0.80	1.20

The assessor's value is $250,000 in examples 1 and 2. The actual selling prices reflect each end of the market value range. The calculated ratios both fall within an acceptable range.

The assessor's values in examples 3 and 4 represent the low and high values in the market value range. The selling prices represent the opposite extremes of the market value range. The results are ratios that fall outside the acceptable levels. The smart assessor will attempt to set values as close to the middle of the market value range to avoid this last example.

Another important part of the property tax system is the mill rate. One **mill** is equal to one dollar of tax for each $1,000 of value. A mill rate of 0.04347826 is equal to approximately $43.48 for each one thousand dollars of valuation. The tax bill for Property 1 above is calculated as:

$$250{,}000 / 1{,}000 = 250$$

$$250 * 43.47826 = \$10{,}869.57$$

The **mill rate** is calculated by dividing the budget amount needed by the total value of all taxable property.

Budget		$100,000
Total taxable value	÷	2,300,000
Mill rate	=	0.04347826

This mill rate then multiplied by the value of individual properties to calculate their tax bill. The process becomes more complicated when the number of local taxing jurisdictions increases and their territories overlap. For instance, a home located within a city may be required to pay taxes to the city, and a school district as well as the county. However, the basic process of calculating a tax bill remains the same.

The Big Shift

The requirement that the owner pay the entire tax bill, or at least one-half of it at one time is one of the greatest problems of the property tax system. That one payment can create a hardship for property owners. That leads to the property tax being the most hated of the three kinds of taxation. In fact, many people pay more in sales and/or income taxes over a year than they pay in property taxes. The difference is their payments on these taxes are spread out in smaller amounts.

People upset with the property tax appeal to their senator or representative to change the property tax system. Sometimes those senators or representatives make changes that make the system more complex and difficult to administer. They have also placed restrictions on the budgeting process. This creates difficulties for people who run local taxing jurisdictions. However, I will focus on the valuation layer of the system. At that level legislative adjustments often frustrate local administrators while doing little to actually ease the property tax burden.

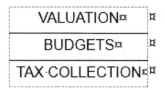

It is important to picture the property tax system as multi-layered. That is because each layer depends on functions conducted in the upper layers. The top layer is where valuation occurs. The next layer is the budgeting layer. The final or bottom layer is the collection layer. Legislation can be directed toward any one or all of these layers, but we will focus our attention on the top.

A common response to property tax complaints has been to apply a different assessment rate by property class. All the properties were assessed at 100% of their market value in the earlier illustration. Under a classification system, they would be assessed at different rates according to a schedule set by the legislature. Below we have an example of the same properties with different assessment rates. The rate for residential properties is 12% and the rate for commercial properties is 25%. The budget amount remains the same.

Property	Market Values	Class	Assessed Value	Mill Rate	Taxes	Difference
1	250,000	0.12	30,000	0.21379	$6,413.70	($4,455.87)
2	125,000	0.12	15,000	0.21379	$3,206.85	($2,227.93)
3	450,000	0.12	54,000	0.21379	$11,544.66	($8,020.56)
4	875,000	0.25	218,750	0.21379	$46,766.56	$8,723.08
5	600,000	0.25	150,000	0.21379	$32,068.50	$5,981.54
Totals	2,300,000		467,750		$100,000.27	

Two new columns have been added to the previous table. A new column has been added to show the Assessed Value. That value is calculated by multiplying the Market Value by the assessment rate shown under the column headed "Class". The column headed "Difference" shows the difference in the amount of taxes paid by each property. Notice that all of the residential property burdens decreased while the tax burden for both commercial properties increased. This different treatment is called a **tax shift**. The total tax burden for the jurisdiction did not change. However, part of the tax burden for residential properties was shifted to commercial properties.

The other significant change is the added requirement to assign and track classes. The new requirement seems simple. A house is a residence and a grocery store is commercial. At its basic level, however, it adds another chance for a clerical error. A clerk could type 0.25 instead of 0.12. It also raises questions about specific properties. For example, how many residential units in the same building are required to change the class from residential to commercial? Or, if I rent my cabin on the lake for the summer, is it residential or commercial? If these aren't answered in the law, they are left to the local assessor and, in some cases, the court system to work out.

Homeowners should also keep in mind that the local grocer whose property taxes increased due to classification has to have money to pay those taxes. Since his primary source of revenue is from the groceries he sells, those prices may have to increase. Therefore, some of that shift in property taxes from residential to commercial may be shifted back to grocery buyers.

The Cap

Another approach lawmakers take is to establish a maximum amount that property values can increase from one appraisal cycle to another. The assessor is required in most states to establish the market value of every property. Placing a maximum amount on increases for tax purposes requires the assessor to track two values for each property. A cap requires the assessor to track both the market and the capped value. This legislation ignores the fact that the real estate market is not just one single market. Values change at different rates over time and for different neighborhoods and property types. The result of applying value caps is a shifting of the tax burden in ways that are nearly impossible to predict. Take the following example.

In the top table, we use the same five properties but apply different rates of change for each to reflect the difference in markets. Starting values are multiplied by the rate of change and then by the appropriate assessment rate to calculate the assessed value. The budget for the entire jurisdiction is left at $100,000 and taxes are calculated on the basis of the assessed values multiplied by the mill rate.

Property	Values	Change	Market	Class	Assessed Value	Mill Rate	Taxes
1	250,000	1.05	262,500	0.12	31,500	0.2013	$6,342.33
2	125,000	1.03	128,750	0.12	15,450	0.2013	$3,110.76
3	450,000	1.10	495,000	0.12	59,400	0.2013	$11,959.82
4	875,000	1.03	901,250	0.25	225,313	0.2013	$45,365.37
5	600,000	1.10	660,000	0.25	165,000	0.2013	$33,221.72
Totals	2,300,000		2,447,500		496,663		$100,000.00

Apply a cap of 5%

Property	Values	Change	Market	Class	Assessed Value	Mill Rate	Taxes	Difference
1	250,000	1.05	262,500	0.12	31,500	0.2056	$6,475.31	$132.98
2	125,000	1.03	128,750	0.12	15,450	0.2056	$3,175.99	$65.23
3	450,000	1.10	472,500	0.12	56,700	0.2056	$11,655.56	($304.26)
4	875,000	1.03	901,250	0.25	225,313	0.2056	$46,316.57	$951.20
5	600,000	1.10	630,000	0.25	157,500	0.2056	$32,376.56	($845.16)
Totals	2,300,000		2,395,000		486,463		$99,999.99	

The bottom table applies the same calculation with one significant difference: changes in value cannot exceed 5%. Therefore, instead of the assessed values for properties 3 and 5 matching those in the top table, they reflect a change of only 5%. This, of course, results in a lower total assessed value figure, which requires a larger mill rate to generate the same total revenue. Despite the higher mill rate, properties 3 and 5 pay less in property tax than if the total change in value had been recognized. That reduction is shifted to properties 1, 2, and 4 whose value changes were less than or equal to the cap of 5%.

	A	B
Budget	$100,000	$100,000
Divided by total assessed value	496,663	486,463
Mill rate	0.2013	0.2056

These are very simple examples that cannot account for increasing operating costs or budget adjustments that may be put in place over time. They do make the point, however, that taxes are not reduced for everyone by requiring arbitrary adjustments to property value. The tax burden is only shifted from one property or group of properties to another in ways that may not be clear. The only way to reduce property taxes across the board is to reduce or eliminate parts of programs within the budgets of the local jurisdiction: think police, fire, street maintenance, public health, etc.

The Job

I don't remember any of my friends in elementary or high school telling me they wanted to be an assessor when they grew up. Most of my colleagues in the field, like me, "fell into the job" instead of seeking it out. Not only did we not know about it, there wasn't a program in our secondary schools to prepare anyone for the job. There is a good reason for that, several in fact.

First and foremost, the position is not held in high esteem because it is seen as political. About one-half of assessors in the United States are elected. That fact places them on the same level as other politicians in the public's mind. Although some states impose education and other requirements to run for office, not all of them do. The same can be said about appointed assessors. One of my favorite stories is about an assessor who was operating a road grader for the highway department the week before he was appointed as assessor. Operating a road grader is a fine vocation. It just doesn't prepare you to appraise a big box retail store.

Second, as we will learn in the following section, some of what the assessor does is little more than clerical. While that is important work, it doesn't require much education or training and is, therefore, dismissed as not very important.

Administrator

The first thing people think about concerning the local assessor is valuation and the administrative part of the job is ignored. However, an office of any size requires the assessor to perform several key functions unrelated to valuation, but absolutely essential to a smooth-running office. In fact, as the office grows in size, the administrative roll takes on greater and greater importance.

One of the most important duties of the local assessor is to meet all required deadlines. That requires a knowledge of those deadlines and the ability to plan and implement all the intermediate steps that must be taken to meet them.

Every local jurisdiction, including cities, counties, townships or special districts, is created by state law. Their existence and the boundaries within which they operate are spelled out in state statutes. The same holds true for officers of those jurisdictions, including the assessor. So, the assessor must be able to read and understand the laws that define his/her job. The alternative is to have them translated into an understandable format by a trustworthy source. Those laws describe what must be done, and when. An assessor who does not understand them cannot do an effective job and is almost certain to eventually break one of them. A clear understanding of those laws makes the assessor a more effective public servant.

That effective service requires the assessor's office to plan and execute the intermediate steps needed to meet those deadlines. That may be simple in a small office where the annual cycle of activity has remained the same for the last decade. It increases in complexity with an increase in the size of the job and changes in the law that inevitably come from the legislature.

The assessor will usually develop a calendar similar to that shown below to help plan the year's activities.

Activity	Deadline	Statute*
Valuation Date	January 1	9-2571
Mail valuation notices	March 1	9-2630
Property owners file appeals	30 days following notice	9-2736
Informal meetings with the assessor	May 15	9-6532
The assessor provides the final decision	May 20	9-6533
Property owner files with appeal board	30 days following the assessor's notice	6-5688
The assessor certifies values to the clerk	June 1	7-1387
Clerk notifies taxing jurisdictions of values	June 15	7-1389
Governing bodies certify budgets to clerk	August 25	7-2534
County clerk certifies tax roll to county treasurer	November 1	7-2535
Tax statements sent by the county treasurer	November 15	7-2649
First half property taxes due	December 20	7-2650

*All numbers are examples only and do not reflect any state statutes

This is a reasonable example of a tax calendar. What it fails to show are the intermediate steps needed. For example, assume the assessor is required to appraise every property in the county each year. In addition to that he has to re-inspect one-sixth of those properties each year. There are 100,000 properties in this county.

The assessor must compare the calendar of assessment functions to the tax calendar. He or she may use a tool called a phase delineation chart that shows when various phases of the valuation effort begin and end.

Phase Delineation Chart												
Phase	Jan	Feb	Mar	Apr	May	Jun	Jul	Aug	Sep	Oct	Nov	Dec
Valuation Complete	▓											
Notice and Appeals			▓	▓								
Sales Data Collection	▓	▓	▓	▓	▓	▓	▓	▓	▓	▓	▓	▓
Field Data Collection						▓	▓	▓	▓			
Neighborhood Delineation								▓				
Land Valuation								▓				
Depreciation Analysis								▓				
Model Development									▓	▓		
Final Valuation											▓	
Value Review												▓

First, the assessor must count on the staff who will be tied up with appeals from shortly after the notices are mailed until the final day of hearings. That means staff will be answering telephone calls and responding to property owners who come to the office. Staff will then schedule and conduct hearings until the results are mailed to the property owners. Clerical staff may handle some of these duties in larger offices. Appraisal staff will still be directly responsible for conducting hearings.

After the hearings are completed, the assessor can send staff to the field. This requires staff members to physically inspect newly constructed buildings, properties that have sold recently, and properties where the owner has been issued a building permit. It may also involve re-inspecting a portion of all properties on a regular schedule. The assessor monitors activity in these areas to take advantage of overlaps and avoid revisiting the same property in the same year. For example, a sale might occur in the part of the county that is being inspected this year. That allows the field worker to verify property characteristics for both the regular file and the sales file with one visit.

Assume the assessor is scheduled to re-inspect 17,000 properties. There are another 5,000 properties on which there is either new construction or a building permit has been issued or it recently sold. That means 22,000 properties have to be inspected this year. However, the assessor doesn't have a year. Five-twelfths of the year has already been used for appeals. Time also has to be set aside at the end of the year to update valuation models, generate values, and review them before January 1.

That may mean the assessor has the three summer months, with possibly one fall month held open, to conduct all fieldwork. There are ninety-two days in the three months of the summer, but the assessor can't count on all of them. There are, depending on the year, 31 weekend days. There is one holiday, July 4th, which may involve more than one day, depending on the year and the jurisdiction policies. In addition, the assessor should allow for some sick time and vacations. The actual number of work days available is much less than the ninety-two.

Total Days	92
Weekend days	-31
Holiday	-1
Sick days	-2
Vacation days	-5
Work days available	54

The calculation now becomes 22,000 properties / 54 days = 407. That final figure represents the number of properties that have to be inspected each day. The following formula is used by the International Association of Assessing Officers to help assessors complete the calculation.

$$S = P / (R \times T)$$

Where:

S = number of staff required

P = number of items to be worked (properties)

R = rate at which each of the items can be processed per the measure of time selected

T = the time period expressed in the unit of time consistent with the rate

To show how this formula works we plug in the numbers from our illustration along with the added assumption that each field worker can inspect 20 properties each day.

S = to be calculated

P = 22,000

R = 20 per day

T = 54 days

S = 22,000 / (20 x 54)

S = 22,000 / 1,080

S = 20.37 or 21

The assessor will need to assign 21 staff members to this field inspection project to complete it in the time allowed. If there are only fifteen (15) staff available, he/she can encourage the staff to produce more in a day.

R = P / T / S

R = rate to be calculated

P = properties to be inspected

T = time period for the project

S = number of staff assigned

R = 22,000 / 54 / 15

R = 27 – *the number of properties to be inspected in one day by each staff member*

In other words, the staff have to inspect 6 more properties each day than they did before.

The assessor could extend the field inspection period another month into September, which would add another 20 days to the total.

S = to be calculated

P = 22,000

R = 20 per day

T = 54 + 20 days = 74

S = 22,000 / (20 x 74)

S = 22,000 / 1,480

S = 14.8 say 15

These are calculations the assessor must make with each new phase of the appraisal process, with little guidance beyond the formula itself. Each part of that formula can be changed, based on the assessor's judgment or required by available resources.

The assessor must determine whether the staff can work harder, faster or smarter and how to motivate them to do it. That involves another area of responsibility - human resources.

Many assessors have moved up the ranks within an assessment office. They may have started their career as a data collector or a personal property clerk. Then they were promoted to supervisor, then to middle management. Finally, they applied for the assessor position and were either appointed or elected to it. Just because a person has moved up the employment ranks in an assessment office doesn't mean he or she is ready to lead it. Lack of human resources skills is quite common in these cases.

I have personally worked in and with counties ranging in size from 25,000 properties to 1 million+. The one thing they all had in common was they used human beings. Assessors in large counties concentrate less on valuation and more on basic staffing issues such as hiring, training, and disciplining staff. Unless the assessor comes to the job with a human relations background or is quick to learn the essentials, he or she may struggle in this area.

Another management responsibility that new assessors struggle with is budgeting. Everything done in an assessment office costs money. Even when staff are doing nothing more than sitting at their desks, they are being paid and that money has to be included in a departmental budget. Beyond salaries, there are expenses for office supplies, travel, training, machine rental or purchase, and possibly outside services such as consulting. All of these, and more, have to be considered by the assessor and included in annual budgets. Previous budgets are helpful unless something or someone changes. That change may come in the form of a statutory change or a change in the governing body that renders large portions of the previous year's budget meaningless.

Valuer

The sole reason for having the position of appraiser/assessor is to appraise property for tax purposes. If the property tax did not exist, there would be no need for the assessor. In the early part of my career, I tried to separate my department from the hated property tax (in vain I might add). The situation would be different if the office of assessor generated appraisals for every real estate transaction in the county, but they don't.

On the other hand, the assessor **is** an appraiser - someone who estimates the value of something. In this case, it is the value of those items the legislature directs him or her to appraise for property tax purposes. The job is the same in some respects as the person who appraises houses for bank loans. Both of them rely on information found in the real estate market and both are trained in using several approaches to estimating the value of something.

By the way, it is important that the reader understands what an appraisal is. For those of us in the appraisal industry, an appraisal, is an *estimate* of value. This value is referred to as *market value*, sometimes fair market value. It is the amount of money that a willing buyer will pay a willing seller for a piece of property on an open market when neither of them is being pressured to buy or sell and both have perfect knowledge of the market. This describes a situation that virtually never occurs in real life. The appraiser uses his or her judgment to find those sales that most closely match that description.

There are some significant differences between a single property appraiser and a mass appraiser (assessor). First, some states require their assessors to value things other than real estate for tax purposes. In some of those instances, the laws require the assessor to value those things at something other than market value. Some items of personal property may be valued using a guide published by the state. In these cases, assessment becomes more of a clerical function, with the assessor looking up personal property items in a guide and copying the value to a list. This activity can be tedious and time-consuming, resulting in pennies of value being chased by dollars of staff time. Since this particular assessment function varies so much from state to state, there aren't national companies willing to devote time to writing software to make the job easier.

The reader should also know the difference between real and personal property. Most people tend to think that everything they own is personal property because they own it. However, that is not the case with appraisers. An appraiser calls anything that is included on the land and improvements to the land as well as all the rights of ownership as real property. Everything else is personal property. Therefore, your house and the lot where it is located is real property and the car in your driveway is personal property, along with your lawn mower, clothes, furniture, jewelry, etc.

The second difference between single property and mass appraisers is in the way they appraise real property. The approaches we will talk about are the same but the quantity is different. A single property appraiser deals with one property at a time. As a result, he or she may appraise between 80 and 100 properties per year. The mass appraiser, in many counties, will appraise every piece of real property in the county every year. In one of the jurisdictions where I worked, we appraised 150,000 residential properties every year.

That can only be accomplished through the effective use of **common data**, **standardized methods** and **statistical testing**. Let me explain what these terms mean.

<u>Common Data</u> - One of the differences between mass and single property appraisers is the timing of the data collection. A single property appraiser will collect all the information needed for the appraisal at the time the appraisal is requested. That information includes a thorough description of the property being appraised (referred to as the subject property), as well as properties used for comparison purposes. It also includes information from the local real estate market. Sale prices will be collected along with the conditions surrounding the sale. Rental rates will be collected when commercial property is being appraised. The appraiser collects any information that might affect the value of the property being appraised. Since the single property appraiser depends on that information to make a living, it is not typically shared with any other appraiser.

The mass appraiser attempts to collect the same information with three major differences. First, every data collector is trained to do their work in the same way, so that the information collected will be equally reliable. Single property appraisers have made great strides in adopting the same property descriptions. However, each appraiser is left to their judgment when asked to evaluate the quality of construction or the extent of depreciation in a structure. Mass appraisers work to match each other's judgment calls to ensure consistency. In other words, every mass appraiser tries to agree on the appropriate rating for every property.

Mass appraisers work hard on consistency because they enter everything into a common file. That includes property characteristics as well as any information they pull from the market. Individual property appraisers tend to keep their property information to themselves. While there may be some limits, virtually every appraiser working for a county has access to that central file.

Another feature of this common data is its maintenance. As stated earlier, the single property appraiser collects property information on the subject and comparable properties at the time of the appraisal. While experienced appraisers will support that as the best approach, it is also expensive and time-consuming. In fact, the single most expensive part of the appraisal effort is the onsite inspection of property. And while every appraiser wants the most current data on the subject property, the fact is real estate doesn't change on its own.

Something or someone has to do something to property to change it. Someone may add a room or remove one; a fire may destroy all or a portion of a house; or the elements may operate to wear away parts of a structure over time, depending on the material used to build it. Because of that, mass appraisers don't have to inspect every property every year as long as there is a re-inspection schedule for all properties over a reasonable time, for example once every six years. It is also helpful if cities within the county share their building permit files to alert the assessor to changes that someone is planning to make to a property. Some states have also passed laws that allow the local assessor to receive such valuable market information as sales transactions and income and expense information.

Standardized Methods – One of my former bosses asked me to find the smallest number of variables needed by an appraisal model to produce a reasonable value. Variables represent something that can change the value of a property. Size, for instance, is an important variable because generally, as the size of a home increases, so does its value. One of the most important variables is the quality rating assigned to a building. This rating attempts to reflect the differences in materials used - wood versus brick exterior walls or asphalt shingles versus slate tiles. It also considers the complexity of the design - a simple rectangle versus several cut-outs and angles. I found this quality rating can account for up to 80% of the difference in value between properties, when translated into a numerical rating.

With this in mind, consistency in quality ratings is essential to the accurate appraisal of buildings. That is easy for the single property appraiser since there is only one appraiser involved. It may also be possible in a mass appraisal setting if the county can effectively do its work with only one person assigning quality ratings. That is rarely possible except in the smallest counties. Where it is not possible, the mass appraiser must emphasize standardization of this rating, and this is not the only instance where it is required.

| Poor Quality | Average Quality | Excellent Quality |

The images above were computer generated and a local jurisdiction would use something similar to train their appraisers.

An efficient assessor's office will separate the steps involved in appraising into clearly defined tasks. Depending on the size and expected length of the task, an individual may be assigned and trained on one or more of them. For example, a large jurisdiction may have staff members whose only task (job) is to collect information in the field. Others will enter that information into a computer. Still, others will develop valuation models that will use the information collected to estimate a new value for each property.

Another difference between a single property appraiser and a mass appraiser is the emphasis on equity. A single property appraiser isn't concerned with whether the value of the subject property is consistent with others up and down the block. On the other hand, a mass appraiser must be concerned with both the value of each property and how that value compares with those of surrounding properties. The consistency implied here can only be achieved using standardized methods.

Statistical Testing – There is an old adage, at times attributed to Mark Twain: "There are three kinds of lies: lies, damned lies, and statistics." One of the reasons people identify with the saying is that statistics have been misused with the people themselves as the victims. So, let's get this out of the way at the very beginning of this discussion – statistics have been misused and can be misleading in the wrong hands. For example, a 2% inflation rate can be used to claim that inflation is increasing since it is greater than zero or decreasing since it is less than it was last month. The best use of statistics is to highlight trends by measuring the same statistic over time; the most reliable interpreter of those trends is someone who states what they are without adding a quality rating to them.

Armed with a thorough understanding of what they represent and in the right hands, statistics can be extremely useful. A mass appraiser can use statistics to monitor the movement and direction of real estate markets. They can be used to point out problems in appraisal and even lead to a resolution of those same problems. Single property appraisers typically do no use statistics to measure their work, because they only appraise one property at a time, and their work is judged using different measures.

The Ratio Study

The primary statistical tool in mass appraisal is the ratio study. It uses three statistics: the median, the coefficient of dispersion and the price related differential. Individually, these three statistics are important, but the complete picture of the quality of the appraisal effort can only be obtained by using all three. We will walk through the calculation and interpretation of each.

Appraised Value / Selling Price = Ratio

Let's begin by describing the ratio we are using. This ratio is calculated by dividing the value estimated by the assessor by the actual selling price of the property. The appraiser/assessor estimates the market value of a piece of property as of a given date. That is important because real estate markets change such that a property may sell for one price on one date and another price at a later date. Since the appraisal is an estimate of the price a property would bring as of a date, it is critical that the sales used to measure that appraisal occurred as close to that date as possible. Otherwise, the ratio of appraisal to selling price will not accurately represent the relationship between the appraisal estimate and the market at that specific point in time.

It is also important that the selling price accurately reflects what is happening in the rest of the market. That means the conditions surrounding the sale must reflect what typically occurs when a person places their property for sale on the open market. Someone buys the property and finances that purchase with a typical loan. When a property is sold because the seller is forced to sell or the buyer is under pressure to buy, that transaction is not typical and therefore does not reflect the rest of the market.

An appraiser tries to learn what patterns exist in the market and replicates them as much as possible. That cannot be done if the sales used in that process do not reflect typical market activity. Likewise, the quality of that appraisal cannot be accurately measured when sales used do not reflect that same market activity.

One final comment has to be made before we go on. The appraisal used in the ratio study must be the final estimate by the appraiser. Building and testing valuation models is an iterative process; it is done over and over again until the appraiser/assessor is satisfied that the results reflect the market. Using a different value than the one certified by the assessor will result in misleading conclusions regarding the quality of the appraisal process.

The Median Ratio

The median is the preferred statistic among the measures of central tendency. These statistics are used to measure the extent to which a set of numerical values group around a central point. The median is a ranking statistic. That means it is found in the middle of a list of numbers that are arranged in the order of their numeric value. For example, if you have five ratios, the median would be the third ratio from the top or the bottom.

Rank	Ratios		Ratios	Rank
1	1.50		0.85	5
2	1.00		0.90	4
3	0.95	Median	0.95	3
4	0.90		1.00	2
5	0.85		1.50	1

When there are an even number of ratios in the list, the two middle ratios are averaged to calculate the median.

Rank	Ratios		Ratios	Rank
1	1.50		0.80	6
2	1.00		0.85	5
3	0.96		0.94	4
4	0.94	(.96 + .94)/2 = .95 = Median	0.96	3
5	0.85		1.00	2
6	0.80		1.50	1

Most people are familiar with the average or mean question of why the mean is not used in ratio studies. The explanation is that the median is not heavily influenced by outliers that occur in the real estate market. Outliers are sales that meet all the requirements for a typical market sale but do not fit the pattern set by the sales of similar properties. It is nearly impossible to exclude all outlier sales from either the appraisal process or its evaluation.

Take for example to two listings above. The median has already been found and the calculation of the mean is very simple.

1.50		
1.00		
.95		
.90		
.85		
5.20	÷ 5 = 1.04	Mean

1.50		
1.00		
.96		
.94		
.85		
.80		
6.05	÷ 6 = 1.06	Mean

Median - .95 versus Mean – 1.04

Median - .95 versus Mean – 1.06

The question for the appraiser is which of these two statistics, the mean or the median, more accurately reflects the middle of the data. The appraiser uses every ratio to calculate the mean. That means it is drawn toward any outliers, such as the 1.50 ratio in each table. The median, on the other hand, does not consider the outliers beyond listing them and therefore is not influenced by them. This has the added benefit of making the median a more stable measure than the mean as ratios are added to the sample. Notice how little the median value changes when ratios are added to each sample.

Rank	Ratios	Rank	Ratios	Rank	Ratios	Rank	Ratios
1	1.50	1	1.50	1	1.60	1	1.60
2	1.00	2	1.00	2	1.50	2	1.50
3	0.95	3	0.95	3	1.00	3	1.00
4	0.90	4	0.90	4	0.95	4	0.95
5	0.85	5	0.85	5	0.90	5	0.90
		6	0.80	6	0.85	6	0.85
				7	0.80	7	0.80
						8	0.75
Median	0.95		0.93		0.95		0.93
Mean	1.04		1.00		1.09		1.04

Because the median is found at the center of the sample, one-half of the ratios are higher than the median and one-half are lower. From an appraisal standpoint, the ideal median is 1.00 or 100%. There are variations in the real estate market that cannot be measured. Because of that most states express the standard for the median as a range from 0.90 to 1.10 (90% - 110%). This means the median is acceptable as long as it falls within that range.

It is very important for the reader to understand that the real estate market is not perfect. When someone goes to the grocery store to buy a can of beans, they know that every can of beans of a given brand is going to be the same price. The same buyer may enter a subdivision of very similar homes, but the sale prices will vary, sometimes substantially. Part of that is due to the negotiating skills of the buyer and seller, but it may also be affected by the time of day, the weather, the relative health of the buyer and seller or just the buyer's taste in wall covering. These are things that neither the single property nor mass appraiser can measure and are therefore referred to as *noise* in the market. That is why measures of appraisal accuracy use ranges rather than single points.

By comparing the appraised value to the actual selling price of a property the ratio is measuring the appraisal level. The assessor wants all appraisals to equal the selling prices. That will place the median ratio equal to 100% (1.00). A median ratio lower than that indicates the appraisals are lower than the selling prices while a median above that indicates appraisals are higher.

Most assessors would be happy with a median ratio of .95 and that is certainly within the acceptable range. However, it doesn't tell the whole story. It indicates that the appraisal level is acceptable, but it says nothing about how much appraisals vary from that median. If every ratio was equal to or only slightly higher or lower than 0.95 the assessor would have done a very good job. On the other hand, if the median is the only ratio that falls within the acceptable range, the quality of the assessor's work is questionable. It will take the coefficient of dispersion to tell us how much variation exists in the appraisals.

The Coefficient of Dispersion

The coefficient of dispersion attempts to measure how much the ratios in a sample of sales vary from the median ratio on the average. It is calculated by

1. finding the difference between the median and every ratio in the sample while ignoring the signs;
2. summing the differences;
3. dividing the sum by the number in the sample to calculate the average; and
4. dividing that result by the median.

The ideal result of an appraisal would be for every appraised value to match that property's selling price. Then the ratio of appraised value to sale price would be 1.00 or 100%. The coefficient of dispersion measures how much the appraisal missed the 100% goal, either higher or lower. The important consideration is the amount of the miss, not whether it was on the low side or the high. That is why the "+" and "-" signs are ignored in part of the calculation.

Ratios	Median	Difference
1.50	- .95 =	.55
1.00	- .95 =	.05
.96	- .95 =	.01
.94	- .95 =	.01
.85	- .95 =	.10
.80	- .95 =	.15
		.87

$$0.87 \div 6 = 0.145$$

$$0.145 \div 0.95 = 0.15 \text{ or } 15\%$$

The total 0.87 is divided by the number in the sample (6) to calculate the average difference of 0.145. This average difference is then divided by the median ratio and the result is expressed as a percentage.

The figure of 0.15 shows that the average difference between each of the ratios and the median is 15%. In other words, all of the ratios vary from the appraisal level of 95% by an average of 15%.

Standards have been set for the coefficient of dispersion (COD). That standard varies according to the property type and its location. Appraising a group of similar houses should be relatively easy. Therefore, the assessor should be able to achieve a COD of 10% or less. Neighborhoods where properties are very dissimilar, for a variety of reasons, are more difficult to appraise. In those neighborhoods, the assessor should be satisfied with a COD as high as 15%.

Some property types are difficult to appraise, increasing the chance for greater variation among the conclusions. Rural residential property as well as all commercial and industrial properties fall in this category. They may see CODs as high as 20%. The only property type that may be higher is vacant lots, whose COD may be as high as 25%.

All these percentage figures represent goals for the assessor to achieve. If they are not achieved the assessor must determine the reasons why and one of the tools the assessor can use is the price related differential.

The Price Related Differential

Having sales in every quality range is a problem for every assessor. Because the quality of a building affects its value, the assessor is charged with applying a quality rating to every building in the jurisdiction. The following is an example of a rating scale that might be used:

Excellent
Very Good
Good
Average
Poor
Fair
Unlivable

The assessor will invariably find that the large majority of the buildings will fall in the Poor to Good ratings. There will be a few in the Fair and Very Good ratings and rarely any in the Excellent or Unlivable ratings. Of course, this same pattern is found in the sales file, which is where the assessor runs into trouble. As will be explained further under the modeling discussion, sales drive market value analysis. The assessor has to work very hard to avoid appraising all properties close to the average value. This is a problem because most of the sales information comes from properties at or close to the "Average" quality rating. That large number of sales will tend to pull the value of the Poor, Fair and Unlivable buildings higher while at the same time pulling the values of the Good, Very Good and Excellent buildings lower. The result may be a Median and/or COD that does not meet the standards. The Price Related Differential helps to diagnose whether this problem exists and how much of a problem it is.

The Price Related Differential is calculated by dividing the Average or Mean of all the ratios by the Weighted Mean. This last statistic is calculated by adding together all the appraised values and selling prices used in the ratio study and dividing the sum of the appraised values by the sum of the selling prices.

Appraised Values	Selling Prices	Ratios
375,000	250,000	1.50
225,000	225,000	1.00
264,000	275,000	0.96
291,400	310,000	0.94
170,000	200,000	0.85
156,000	195,000	0.80
1,481,400	1,455,000	6.05

The Mean is equal to 6.05 / 6 = 1.01

The Weighed Mean is equal to 1,481,400 / 1,455,000 = 1.02

The Price Related Differential is the equal to 1.01 / 1.02 = 0.99

The usual tendency in mass appraisal is to over-value lower priced properties relative to higher priced properties. That will result in a Price Related Differential (PRD) greater than 1.00; and the stronger that tendency the higher that number. In a similar fashion, if higher value properties are being over-valued relative to lower value properties, the PRD will be less than 1.00 and the stronger that tendency the lower that number.

As with the Median and the COD, the standard for the PRD is expressed as a range, in this case .98 to 1.03. Our example shows a slight tendency to over-value the higher priced properties relative to the lower priced properties. However, the PRD still falls within the acceptable range of 0.98 to 1.03.

Highest and Best Use

Before an appraiser can begin to estimate the value of any piece of real estate, he/she must determine what is called its highest and best use. This is the use that is legal, physically possible and will yield the highest return to the prospective buyer. As you can imagine, this is relatively easy to do in 98%+ of the cases. A house in a subdivision of similar houses, a commercial building located on main street or a farm in an agricultural area are going to be valued just as they are, a house, a commercial building and a farm. Where this determination becomes crucial is when current uses change or the buyer is contemplating a change. For example, a couple owns a farm located on the outskirts of a city. They retire from farming and begin to sell pieces of the farm for commercial use until the only piece remaining contains the homestead. This homestead is now surrounded by commercial property. The highest and best use of that remaining plot of land could very well be commercial rather than residential. Once an appraiser makes that determination, the land value will likely increase from residential to commercial levels. At the same time, the residence will decrease in value as a mis-improvement on a commercial plot. So, it is in those areas where change is occurring that the highest and best determination is most critical to the final value estimate.

Three Approaches to Value

There are three approaches to estimating the value of any property. Both the individual property appraiser and the mass appraiser use one or all three of the approaches to estimate the value of property. These three approaches arc the cost, comparable sales, and income approaches. In theory, an appraiser should be able to apply all three approaches to every property. In reality, their usefulness depends on the type of property being appraised and the availability of market data.

The Cost Approach

The cost approach involves estimating the cost of replacing something that was built on a piece of land. Normally that will be a house or some type of commercial building. The replacement will either be exactly like the building being replaced or will have the same usefulness (utility). The difference relates to the type of property being appraised and the reason for the appraisal. Building materials and techniques have changed over time. That means a building like a five-hundred-year-old church may require the assessor to estimate the cost of reproducing an exact replica. Most appraisals the assessor performs, however, estimate the cost of replacing buildings with something having the same utility as the building being appraised, but constructed using modern materials and construction techniques.

Estimating replacement cost is made easier using cost tables that are divided by quality rating, type of construction, and size ranges. These tables may be created by the assessor, a state agency, or a nationally recognized company. Because of the necessity and difficulty in keeping these tables up to date, many assessors rely on cost manuals generated by a nationally recognized company.

Ease of use makes the cost approach the most universally available to the appraisal process of the three approaches. The assessor attempts to match the quality of the property being appraised with a description in the cost manual being used. Then the base cost is found under the column heading corresponding to that property's construction type and the appropriate size range. It's called a base cost because other items such as heating and cooling equipment, floor covering, garage space, finished basement, etc. are added to it. The number and type of those additions will depend on the manual being used and the appraisal assignment. An individual property appraiser may attempt to assign a cost to an item that adds little to the overall cost, while the local assessor may ignore it or simply note that it exists.

When the assessor uses a nationally developed cost manual, more steps are required to complete the replacement cost estimate. Because the manual is nationally developed, the assessor must adjust the costs for his or her location and the date of the appraisal. Costs from the manual reflect a certain part of the country and a location adjustment has to be made when that is different than the location of the appraised property. Items such as transportation charges, and wage rates vary from one part of the country to another and the appraiser has to account for those differences. Cost manuals are generally not updated completely every year. That means some of the costs must be adjusted for market changes that have occurred since that portion of the manual was last updated.

After the assessor has estimated the cost new of the property being appraised, that cost must be reduced to account for each of three different kinds of depreciation.

First and foremost, there is the natural wear and tear that occurs over time. Every structure will wear out over time and deteriorate to the point that its very existence on the property is a detriment to the total property value. The rate that occurs will vary with the type of construction and local conditions. A masonry structure will not deteriorate as fast as a wooden structure and any structure in a mild climate will outlast one that faces extremes of heat and cold and/or wet and dry. The assessor tries to capture that in the physical condition rating as well as when constructing a **physical depreciation** table.

Another factor that acts to reduce the value of property is a change in market tastes. These changes affect how well given styles function within those markets. To use an extreme example, in the early part of the last century the existence of indoor bathrooms was not common in residential properties. Instead of adding another room to the house, many people chose to cut an area out of an existing room to accommodate these facilities. Sometimes this required occupants to walk through a bedroom to get to the bathroom, which would not be acceptable today. Another example of what the appraiser calls **functional obsolescence** is the absence of any type of air conditioning in a hot climate or adequate heating in a cold one. In any event, the appraiser/assessor must account for these conditions through an appropriate reduction in value.

Finally, the appraiser must account for possible conditions outside the property that may hurt its value. One example used to illustrate this is a slaughterhouse being constructed next to a residential property. That would obviously cause a reduction in the value of the residence even though it's not on the property itself. Appraisers refer to this as **economic obsolescence.** When it is found the appraiser/assessor has to reduce the value of affected properties. He or she must determine how much impact there is and which properties are affected.

The assessor has to identify the depreciation and to assign a dollar amount to it. It is relatively easy to see that depreciation exists. It is much more difficult to assign a dollar amount to take away from the replacement cost estimate. Most cost manuals have suggested physical depreciation tables that are helpful. They cannot account, however, for owner maintenance that was done to halt or slow that depreciation. Remodeling may remove some physical depreciation and all of the functional obsolescence. It is up to the assessor to assign a dollar amount of difference the project made.

The best way for the appraiser to value anything is to find two properties that are alike in every way but one and that have sold recently. The difference in selling price will help establish the dollar value of that one item. For example, assume two houses (A and B) were built at the same time and had the same problem with bathroom placement described above. Assume also that both recently sold after owner A corrected that problem through a remodel. If house A sold for $225,000 and B sold for $220,000, the appraiser can assume that the difference was because of the bathroom issue. The dollar difference of $25,000 may be the amount of functional obsolescence in house B due to the bathroom issue. I emphasize "*may*" because there can be several reasons for the difference and only a group of sales that showed a similar difference in selling price will verify the accuracy of the assessor's assumption.

In theory, an analysis of sales that are grouped by quality rating and age should, in theory, reflect the normal depreciation rate. In other words, we would expect the value of the property to drop off at a fairly smooth rate till it reached the end of the economic life of the structure.

Economic life is a term used to describe how long a structure will continue to be useful in the same manner and extent as other similar structures. For wood frame houses, that is typically 60 years. This is a "rule of thumb", not set in stone.

The graph below reflects what I have found in virtually every analysis of sales to establish or validate a depreciation schedule. The analysis begins by subtracting land value from the most recent selling price of a property and the result is divided by the replacement cost new. This gives a percentage that represents the percent good or the amount of value left in the structure at the time of the sale. It is the opposite of depreciation and it is anticipated to drop from 100% down to near zero at 60 years. This is represented by the solid line, while the figures from the existing table are represented by the dashed line.

Each of these sales is represented on a graph as a single dot and a line that most closely matches the pattern created by those dots is drawn on the graph. The chart below shows what a typical line has looked like in my experience. Instead of being a smooth line that drops off at the beginning and then curves to almost a straight line at 60 years, there is a flattening or even a reversal of direction between 25 and 35 years. Further investigation of the sales revealed that owners tended to remodel and redecorate homes during that time. That action effectively halted or reversed the rate of depreciation for a time.

When appraisers encounter this situation, they respond by lowering the effective age of the structure. This does not ignore the fact that all structures wear out, but recognizes that the extent of remodeling done has extended the useful life of the structure. They make a judgment that the structure that has a chronological (actual) age of 30 years is more similar to structures that are younger, say 25 years. So, they reduce the effective age to 25 and begin the depreciation from that point.

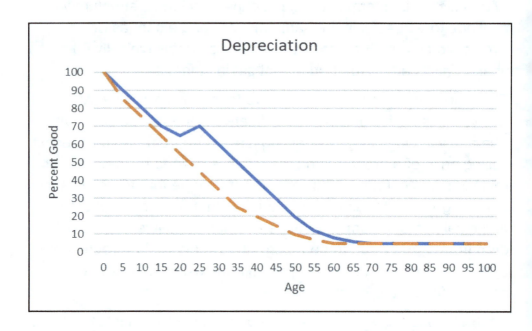

The typical home owner who has not remodeled their home will expect it to depreciate with age. That means they would expect the percent good (opposite of depreciation) to decrease or the amount of depreciation to increase. Therefore, the appraiser will consider the current schedule more or less validated because the solid line, which reflects the current table, lies close to the dashed line, which represents sales data.

The appraiser will have to account for functional and/or economic obsolescence on an individual property basis. They represent situations that are at most unique to a single neighborhood within the jurisdiction. Many times, they effect only one or two properties, which makes attempting to create tables a waste of time. So, they are dealt with one property at a time.

The final step in the cost approach is to add a value for the land. Estimating that value is difficult for both the individual property appraiser and the assessor. It is especially difficult in parts of the county that have been built up for some time. The best approach to estimating that value is through the use of comparable sales. In a fully developed neighborhood, there may not be any sales of vacant land. That forces the assessor to look for sales in areas that are similar to the subject property's neighborhood. Of course, that raises the questions of what constitutes "similar" and how far from the subject property is it reasonable to look? There is no easy answer to either one of those questions, but the assessor should be prepared to support his/her decision.

The cost approach is the most common approach to estimating value of the three. It is usually implemented through the use of a manual or through tables within a computer assisted mass appraisal (CAMA) software system. The remaining two approaches are more property specific in that they are applicable to certain types of property, while the cost approach may be used on any type of property except vacant land.

Below is an example of a simplified cost approach.

Item	Units	Per Unit	Cost
Base Price	1,186	112	132,832
Minimal Basement Finish	1,086	61	66,246
Attached Garage	494	50	24,700
Replacement Cost New			223,778
Physical Deterioration			0
Functional Obsolescence			0
Economic Obsolescence			0
Total Depreciation			0
Depreciation Amount			62,658
Replacement Cost New Less Depreciation			161,120
Land Value	8,773	4.14	36,320
Total Cost Estimate			197,440

The Sales Comparison Approach

For years as a young appraiser, I heard this approach referred to as the "market approach". That fell out of favor because all three approaches are supposed to be driven by market information, which was when the name was changed to the sales comparison approach. However, you may still find some appraisers/assessors referring to it as the market approach to value.

This approach appears deceptively simple: find sales of three to five houses like the property being appraised (subject property) and use their selling prices to estimate the value of the subject. During several discussions with friends concerning their newly assessed value, they will say something like "there are properties like mine all through my neighborhood". The problem is they didn't sell in the last few years.

While, unlike single property appraisers, assessors should consider whether all similar properties in a neighborhood are being appraised at similar values, the best evidence is an actual sale. When a property owner makes the argument that "my house is appraised too high" in relation to neighboring houses, he or she is effectively saying the assessor appraised all those other houses accurately, but made a mistake on mine. A stronger argument would be that a house very similar to mine sold recently for a much lower amount than my appraisal.

Let's consider some of the issues that complicate this approach and begin with the availability of sales. It would make the assessor's job much easier if every property owner in the jurisdiction would sell his/her property during every appraisal cycle. That would provide solid evidence for both the assessor and the owner concerning the value of each property. Unfortunately, property owners (including me) do not want to do that. In fact, like me, they tend to hang onto their property for years and years, possibly leaving the sale of the property to their heirs. I don't know how many people are like me, but the fact is people buy and sell property at different times and for vastly different reasons that don't necessarily follow a pattern.

All this means that it is impossible to predict with any degree of accuracy how many and which properties will sell during a given time period. The challenge for the appraiser is to find those three to five perfectly comparable sales among those properties that actually did sell. Or, in the alternative, to find sales of properties that are enough similar to the subject that they do not require much of an adjustment.

In theory, an appraiser, single property or mass, should be able to adjust the selling price of any sale property for differences between it and the subject to make it a valid comparable sale. The problem is everything works in theory, but not necessarily in practice.

First, what do we mean by adjustment? Most people would agree that the property most comparable to the subject property would be the subject property itself. If the subject sold very near the appraisal date, it would be reasonable to use its selling price as the basis for the appraisal. Since this rarely happens, the appraiser must look for sales that have the same or most of the same characteristics as the subject property, such as size, story height, style, type of construction, number of rooms and lot size. Then the appraiser adjusts the selling price of that comparable up or down for the differences in those same characteristics. For example, an adjustment made for differences in size might proceed as follows:

Size of subject	1,200
Size of comparable sale	1,500
Difference	-300
Typical sale price per square foot	$150
Amount of adjustment	-$45,000

The next question the appraiser must answer after determining the amount of the adjustment is whether it should be positive or negative. The answer depends on whether the particular characteristic being considered typically adds to or subtracts from the selling price. In most cases, a property increases in value with an increase in size, which means the 1,500 square foot property will be more valuable than the 1,200 square foot property. An appraiser would expect its selling price would be higher than what the subject property would bring, in this case, by $45,000. The purpose of the adjustment is to make the comparable sale identical to the subject, which means the appraiser must subtract $45,000 from the comparable property's selling price.

The appraiser must determine which characteristics will be used in the adjustment process. Some, such as size, age, location and quality of construction are very apparent, but it become less obvious and the adjustment process more difficult as the appraiser moves on to other characteristics. For example, the appraiser should obviously make adjustments for the lack of adequate bathroom facilities in a modern home. It is less obvious and more problematic that an adjustment is necessary for the absence of a ventilation fan in that bathroom.

Finally, the appraiser must determine the type of adjustment to be made. The adjustment for size differences is made by comparing the numerical difference between the sale and the subject property. The difference in square footage is then used along with the selling price per square foot to calculate an adjustment. The same approach can be used for items such as age. On the other hand, the presence or absence of a fireplace may result in a lump sum being added to or subtracted from the comparable selling price.

To estimate the amount of the adjustment the appraiser must perform what is called a "paired sales analysis". In its pure form, this requires the appraiser to find two sale properties that are identical in every respect but for the particular property characteristic being analyzed. For example, if we want to know how much a fireplace adds to the value of a house, we would find two sales that have identical characteristics except for the fact that one has a fireplace and the other does not. Then the difference in selling prices will equal the contributory value of the fireplace, or how much value a fireplace adds to a home.

Similar to the problem of finding a sale that exactly matches the subject property, finding two sales like those described above is difficult. At times the appraiser will have to make other adjustments before accounting for the value of the fireplace. For example, one of the two sales may have occurred back in time requiring the appraiser to adjust for market differences that have occurred. The selling price will have to be adjusted according to the increase or decrease in prices of similar properties that have occurred since the time of the sale, or the conclusion will not accurately reflect the contribution of that fireplace. As the differences mount up the complexity of the appraisal problem increases along with the uncertainty of the conclusions. A lot depends on the judgment of the individual appraiser and his or her ability to spot patterns in the data.

The mass appraiser uses statistical tools such as multiple regression analysis to help him or her identify patterns of relationships within the property characteristics of sales. The most experienced and knowledgeable users of such tools will produce the most reliable results, naturally, and just as naturally, not every member of every assessor's office staff will have that expertise. In fact, there may only be one or two people on staff who are relied upon to help the remaining staff establish those relationships and present them in the form of valuation models, which we will discuss shortly.

Before we discuss market modeling, it is important for the reader to understand and appreciate the difficulty any appraiser faces in acquiring market data of any kind. I was very fortunate to work in the State of Kansas where the County Appraisers Association was able to convince the legislature to pass a law requiring the disclosure of sales information to local county appraisal officials. Before the passage of that law, appraisal offices were scrounging for sales data using every source we could lay our hands on, from newspaper ads to real estate fliers to word of mouth on the street.

You can imagine this kept one or more staff members busy all the time and the results were not always reliable. A real estate flier may list an asking price that is different than the final sale. In today's market that asking price is just as likely to be lower than the final sale price than higher. This translates into staff time invested and taxpayer dollars spent on a project that yields questionable results but still represents the norm in many assessment jurisdictions. Allowing assessors access to sales information will require a change in state statutes that many legislators are not ready to make.

Finding sales is difficult enough. Unless the appraiser has some way of being notified when a property sells, he or she has to undertake the type of search described above. But the process doesn't end there. You might think a sale is a sale and that everyone found will be used, but that isn't the case.

First, some transactions are not sales. Trades are a good example where one property or a portion of it is traded for something else. An owner may simply change the name on a title or otherwise alter the ownership interest that affects the deed and it shows up as a transaction in the county clerk's office.

Sales of single-family residential property are usually straightforward. However, even there the appraiser may find a transfer between relatives that doesn't fit the pattern in the local market. I probably wouldn't sell my home to one of my daughters at a price approaching market rates. Likewise, a lending institution does not need to recover any more than the amount of the loan, which is likely equal to the original selling price minus the down payment. Each of these situations and more have to be evaluated on their own merits before the sale can be used for appraisal purposes.

Sales of rural properties present their own challenges. A small rural homesite can be compared to nearby suburban sites. But a home sitting among other structures used to support a farming operation that includes several agricultural acres requires the appraiser to estimate the contributory value of the home to the entire operation. The latter resembles a commercial enterprise more than a residential property.

Commercial and industrial sales present the greatest challenge to the appraiser because it is rare that the sale is limited to real estate. Often the sale will include personal property, inventory, machinery and equipment and the elusive component of business value or goodwill. If a sale is to be used, the appraiser has to separate each of these pieces and accurately determine their contribution to the total selling price. The difficulty in doing that causes many appraisers to discount the sales comparison approach when valuing that type of property in favor of either the cost or income approaches.

CHARACTERISTIC	SUBJECT	COMPARABLE #1		COMPARABLE #2		COMPARABLE #3	
Address	400 W Morse	502 E Grant		350 W Jackson		460 W Lee	
Sale Price		$300,000		$236,000		$235,000	
Sale Price/Gross Liv Area		$72		$102		$80	
VALUE ADJUSTMENTS	ITEM	ITEM	± Adjustment	ITEM	± Adjustment	ITEM	± Adjustment
Sale Date		3 months		2 months		3 months	
Site	15205 sf	32164 sf	-14,415	9800 sf	4,594	13200 sf	1,704
Style	Ranch	Ranch		Ranch		Ranch	
Quality of Construction	Average	Average		Average		Average	
Chronological Age	11	24	2,000	0		3	
Room Count	13/5/3.0	8/3/2.0	2,000	8/3/2.0	2,000	8/4/3.1	-1,000
Gross Living Area	2862 sf	4176 sf	-19,710	2310 sf	8,280	2995 sf	-1,395
Finished Basement Living Area	0	0		0		0	
Heating and Cooling	Central	Central		Central		Central	
Garage/Carport	2 Car Att	2 Car Att		None	4,000	2 Car Att	
Net Adjustment			-30,125		18,874		-691
Adjusted Sale Price			$269,875		$254,874		$234,309

The Income Approach

The reason there are three approaches to estimating the value of real estate is that buyers and sellers have different motivations for involvement in that market. Builders and developers use the RCN (Replacement Cost New) of the cost approach to help establish the profitability of a proposed project. Insurers may use the DEP (accumulated depreciation) to determine what part of an insurance claim will be paid. Realtors track the selling prices of homes to help them determine what asking price is reasonable. In addition, buyers

52

in the commercial market want to know how much income a property can be expected to generate over its useful life.

The income approach is best used in those instances when the buyer is interested in both a return **on** and a return **of** the investment. In other words, the buyer wants to earn money on the property while it is owned and sell it for at least the amount of the initial purchase price. That could apply to any type of property but the income approach is more often used to value commercial properties such as a retail store or an office building.

Because the emphasis is on the income-producing capabilities of the property, the assessor has to convert income into value. That is done using what is called a capitalization rate. This is a percentage figure that reflects the relationship between a property's income and its value. We learned in basic math that if the result of multiplying **A** times the percentage figure **B** results in figure **C**, then we can recalculate figure **A** by dividing figure **C** by percentage figure **B**.

If

$A = 100,000$

$B = 0.10$

$A \times B = C = 10,000$

Then

$$100,000 \times 0.10 = 10,000$$

$$10,000 \div 0.10 = 100,000$$

The assessor's job is to find **A** using figures **B** and **C**.

The "C" portion of this formula represents the net operating income (NOI) of the subject property. This is the typical income for the type of property being appraised less typical operating expenses. It is only by chance that it would be the current owner's actual net income because the assessor must determine what the real estate market indicates the typical income for this type of real property would be. And we are only considering the income that would be received from renting the building. To consider all the owner's income might include items that do not relate to just the building. For example, if the owner of the building also operated a business within that same building, the total income would include profit or loss from the business. In addition, because the business owner also owns the building, the total income would naturally not include rent.

The job of the assessor is to determine what the market indicates the subject building would generate in rent under typical management. This requires the assessor to observe several commercial properties and their operation. Some will be well managed while others will suffer from poor management. The assessor has to be able to determine whether and to what extent the income from the property is being affected by the management practices of the owner. This will help establish what the assessor refers to as typical market rental rates for the type of property being appraised.

The assessor must identify those items on the owner's expense report that are necessary to the operation of the building. A management fee that is typical for the type of building being appraised is acceptable, while mortgage payments are not. Commercial buildings need to be managed and assessors should anticipate a reasonable fee attached to that service. On the other hand, whether a building carries a mortgage and how much it is directly tied to a particular owner. Depreciation might be shown on the owner's report but not included by the assessor because it doesn't directly relate to the operation of the building and the production of income.

As you can see from this brief discussion, this type of analysis requires a great deal of experience in the commercial real estate market. If the local assessor does not have that experience, it should be obtained from one of several different sources.

The capitalization (cap) rate is the most difficult and controversial piece of the income formula. The previous discussion showed that the cap rate can be obtained from sales of commercial buildings whose net operating income figures are available. The assessor uses the net operating income and sale price figures and plugs them into the math formula as shown below.

Net Operating Income		$10,000
Sale Price	÷	$100,000
Indicated Cap Rate	=	0.10

Problems begin with the sale price and the questions discussed earlier concerning what it includes. Assuming there are a sufficient number of good sales, the assessor must select operating expenses from the income and expense reports of those properties. The objective is to identify typical expenses for every type of commercial property in the county. This is virtually impossible in counties that do not have a large number of commercial properties and an expert staff. It is only marginally better in counties that have a large number of commercial properties. That is because property owners are hesitant to turn over their information to government employees.

In many cases this forces local assessors to contract for the work or rely on studies conducted by outside firms. This contributes to the controversy surrounding the selection of a cap rate. On the other hand, the other side in a valuation appeal will face the same, if not greater, obstacles. In the final analysis, the income approach estimate is typically placed alongside the cost estimate, with the final value estimate left to the judgment of the assessor. That judgment is based in large part on the amount of support that exists for one over the other.

Models and Modeling

When most people hear the words model or modeling, they immediately think about someone like Cindy Crawford or maybe that model car or model airplane they put together as a kid. In each case, one thing is supposed to represent something else. Runway models are supposed to reflect how every woman wants to, or is supposed to want to, look like. A model car or airplane is a scaled-down version of the "real life" car or plane.

When assessors talk about modeling, they are talking about mathematical formulas. These formulas are designed to represent a pattern within the real estate market. Mathematical formulas don't have to be multi-variable mathematical monsters created and used by math geniuses. In reality, every appraiser uses models in various forms in all three approaches to value. A mathematical formula is another way of representing relationships in the market.

The cost approach is a good example. If you remember from the previous discussion, we begin by estimating the current cost to replace a structure. We subtract from that figure any depreciation and finally add a land value. That process can be expressed as follows:

$$(RCN - DEP) + LAND = COST$$

Where:

RCN = Replacement cost new

DEP = Depreciation

Land = Land value

Each of the three components above can be broken down further into their own individual formulas. Some computer-assisted mass appraisal software systems do just that. Computers, as fast as they are, work faster using formulas than having to look up items in the tables you might find in a printed cost manual.

The comparable sales approach was described as using the selling prices of three to five comparable sale properties to estimate the value of the subject property. This might be expressed as a formula like the following:

$$V_s = S_c \pm Adj_c$$

Where:

V_s = Value of the subject property

S_c = Sale price of each comparable property

Adj_c = Adjustment required for each comparable sale

Finally, the income approach formula in its simplest form is shown below:

$$V = \frac{I}{R}$$

Where:

V = Value of the subject property

I = Net operating income

R = Capitalization rate

In every case, these models can be expanded and expressed in various forms. Each of the components may be broken down further and more variables introduced. But the goal is the same in every case – reflect patterns observed in the real estate market that support an estimate of market value. If the result of implementing any model is something other than market value, it is a failure, no matter how sophisticated or impressive it may be.

Most states require the assessor to notify property owners of any change in the appraised value of their property, usually through a mailed notice. They are then allowed to contest that value through a defined appeal process. The focus of that appeal process has changed over the years from an emphasis on equity for all to an emphasis on resolving individual grievances.

The property tax system is grounded on the assumption that equity among property owners is achieved when everyone is appraised at the market value of their individual properties. With that in mind, the assumption has been that the assessor has achieved that equity, and any movement away from the original estimate of value may create inequity. That is why property owners had the burden of proving the assessor's value was in error.

In recent years some jurisdictions have moved the initial burden of proof to the assessor, which means in a hearing situation the assessor must present evidence supporting the value. There is no assumption of accuracy. The practical effect is to slow the hearing process because the only way the burden doesn't then pass to the property owner is if the assessor fails to present anything, and unfortunately many owners fail to present anything substantive.

At this point, there is a temptation to ask the assessor why he/she clings so tightly to the original value estimate. Why not just give the property owner the lower value they want?

The truth is there is a certain amount of pride on the part of the assessor. After all a great deal of effort has been expended to reach this point. The people who hired or elected the assessor want to feel confident in his or her capabilities and they might lose some of that confidence if appeals are not contested.

There are other reasons to contest value changes. For example, most states have an oversight agency at the state level that requires local assessors to meet certain standards. Those standards usually include meeting the ratio study standards discussed earlier, which has the potential to involve any parcel that is involved in a hearing. In addition, state statutes typically set deadlines for completion of the hearing process, which can, when there are a large number of appeals, push the assessment staff to the default position of denying changes.

There is another reason to contest changes on appeal that goes back to the very reason for relying on market value and that is equity. If the assessor grants a value change that is not justified, it creates inequity in the assessment roll. As a practical matter, it also causes a portion of the property tax burden of the appealed property to be redistributed to every other property in that jurisdiction. As an officer within the property tax system, the assessor should be aware of that and must minimize it as much as possible.

Some Property Owner Questions and Assessor Responses

Why is my house appraised higher than every other house on the block when they are all the same?

Check the assessor's record on your property. There is probably some difference noted on that record that causes your house to be valued differently.

The assessor very likely used a valuation model to estimate the value of your house. That model works by multiplying a value rate by a given property characteristic. For example, the model will multiply a certain rate times the number of square feet of living space in the house:

Value = Rate x Square Feet of Living Area

Value= $50 x 1,250

Value = $62,500

The same process will be repeated for other property characteristics and the results will be added together to produce the final value estimate. When the number of square feet in your house is different than the surrounding houses, that difference will produce a different value. Ask the assessor for a copy of the report they have on your house and check that figure along with all other characteristics to ensure they are correct.

Why did my value increase when I didn't do anything to my property?

Changes in the market value of a property don't depend on physical changes to the property. That value depends on what buyers are paying and sellers are receiving for properties similar to yours in the real estate market.

Another possible reason is the assessor discovered and corrected an error on your property record. The upper floor living area may have been mistakenly coded as an attic, for example. Ask the assessor's office for a printed copy of your property record and check it for yourself. Some of the fields on this record may be coded, so it will be necessary for you to sit with a member of staff to get an explanation.

How can you appraise my property when no one has physically visited it for two years?

Most states require an initial physical inspection of each property during a total reassessment. Single property appraisers conduct these inspections at the time of the appraisal. However, requiring assessors to inspect every property annually can be overly time-consuming and costly. An exception to this rule occurs when an assessor is specifically notified about changes to a property. Buildings do not spontaneously grow or shrink; the only changes they undergo without external intervention are due to physical deterioration. This deterioration happens gradually, allowing it to be monitored through a re-inspection cycle every four to six years. Property owners who have questions about the accuracy of their assessments should review their records, paying particular attention to the amount of depreciation that has been applied to the property.

Why did the assessor's office rely on that one sale in our neighborhood that everyone knows was involved in a bidding war and was overpriced?

There is an often-repeated phrase used in assessor training: "One sale doesn't make a market". The logic behind the statement cuts both ways. A lower-than-market sale can bring values down just as an above-market sale can increase them, which is why the assessor invests so much time in analyzing sales. On the other hand, an assessor ignores those extreme sales at the risk of them being included in a ratio study that a state oversight agency uses to evaluate his or her performance.

My point is that the assessor cannot ignore those sales because the market will not. A realtor operating in that part of the jurisdiction will consider it when a new client wants to sell a house. Likewise, sellers may give it a lot of consideration when they put their home on the market.

While these are reasons for the assessor acknowledging that sale, ask whether and how it was used to value your house. Its existence doesn't automatically mean it had any impact on the value of your house.

Was it used as one of the comparable sales in your valuation? If so, how much was the price adjusted?

The assessor is only interested in raising more money for the county.

There are at least two ways this concern misses the point. First, most assessors I have known simply wanted to do their jobs, earn their paychecks, and go about their lives like everyone else. Those who tried to work the system usually adjusted values one property at a time to lower the taxes of particular individuals to gain their favor, rather than raise the taxes of a group. On the other hand, there are guardrails within the system that tend to keep value changes within certain boundaries. One of those is the state oversight agency which, depending on the state, has powers ranging from a slap on the wrist to withholding monies or even removing the assessor when values fail to meet certain standards. The other is the group of politicians the assessor depends on for local guidance and possibly funding.

Let me say at the very beginning of this discussion that I respect and admire anyone who runs for election to any office. The benefits of doing so are almost entirely personal in the form of satisfying a need to serve, but the disadvantages and headaches far outweigh them. The problem for the assessor is that few, if any, persons come to local offices with an understanding of how the property tax system works. What they do understand are complaints by taxpayers and they want them to stop. So, the second guardrail against assessors' drastically increasing values is the group of local officials who don't want to listen to taxpayer complaints.

The final way in which this concern misses the point is that the tax bill received by a taxpayer may have little to do with the actions of the assessor. Take the two examples below:

Example 1: Mill rate increases at cost of living (3%)					Change
Assessed Value	$50,000	$50,000	$50,000	$50,000	$50,000	0.00%
Mill Rate	0.0435	0.0448	0.0461	0.0475	0.0489	12.41%
Tax Bill	$2,175	$2,240	$2,305	$2,375	$2,445	12.41%
Change		3.0%	2.9%	3.0%	2.9%	

Example 2: Value changes by 25% every year					
Assessed Value	$50,000	$62,500	$78,125	$97,656	$122,070	144.14%
Mill Rate	0.0435	0.0348	0.0278	0.0223	0.0178	-59.08%
Tax Bill	$2,175	$2,175	$2,171	$2,177.73	$2,172.85	-0.10%
Change		0.0%	-0.1%	0.3%	-0.2%	

In the first example, the value of the property does not increase at all for five years. However, because the mill rate increases at a rate of 3% per year, compounded, the total tax increase for the five years is over 12%. In the second example, the property value increases 144% over the five years and the amount of property taxes paid decreases. The point is the property tax bill is dependent on several different things and the value estimated by the assessor is only one.

Property is appraised for the sole purpose of distributing the total property tax burden. Our ancestors decided that fairness and equity would be achieved in the property tax system when every property is appraised at its market value. Persons owning more valuable property would pay more than those owning less valuable property. The tax amount that is to be distributed is determined by someone else.

Politician

Whether they are elected or appointed, an assessor has to be a politician, because he is involved in the process of governing a local county, i.e. politics. Some enjoy the give and take involved in politics and those who head very large counties are some of the best politicians there are. They have to be to hold onto their position beyond one term. That doesn't mean they engage in the type of behavior that has given politics a bad name, under-the-table deals, or lowering the values of their friends' properties. It is because of their ability to work with other politicians that some of the best property tax legislation has been passed and some of the worst has been avoided.

The Kansas County Appraisers Association worked with the realtors' association and some state legislators. Together they convinced the legislature to pass a law that allowed county appraisers to receive information about every sale passing through the Register of Deeds office. That same group went back to the legislature to make sure property owners interested in appealing their property's value had the same access. The first helped every county appraiser do a better job and the second helped avoid a situation where property owners would have been at a disadvantage in an appeal situation. Both instances were the result of appraisers acting as politicians in a political arena.

The assessor should also educate the public about the property tax system and the probable results of changing it. The example above shows when appraisers (assessors) were able to sell the legislature on the benefits of a change in the system. More often than not, local assessors have attempted to discourage changes when it was clear the results would not match the intentions. In many cases, the results would simply shift the tax burden, without resolving the underlying issues.

Commissioners and the Budget

There are many different forms of local government around the country, but the one I will focus on here is the one where a state is divided into several different subdivisions called counties and these counties are led by a board of county commissioners. As I have said before, I have the greatest respect for anyone who seeks public office, and that holds just as true for county commissioners. That doesn't, however, mean that I don't hold them accountable for making bad decisions. After all, they represent the common man, the voter, whose only contact with the government, at any level may have been the annual payment of income tax and renewing their car tags. Most commissioners enter office with the same exposure and level of knowledge. The good ones will proactively try to learn how the county operates and how it should operate. The poor ones will simply react to each new situation with no more information than when they were elected.

These are not bad people and they generally try to do a good job for the public they serve. The fact that they are ignorant of how the property tax system should and does work is not meant to put them down. Over 90% of the adult population doesn't know how the property tax system works. We shouldn't be surprised when some of them are elected to office. The problems come from those who refuse to learn.

Politicians who operate without a broad understanding of the property tax system, tend to act like firefighters stamping out hotspots. Each situation is resolved in a way that is unique to the problem, rather than as part of an overall strategy. Classification is a good example. Residential property owners represent the single largest segment of the voting public and their property taxes are always "*too high*". One approach to resolve that problem has been to assess residential property at a lower level. That shifts some of the tax burden to commercial and/or industrial properties. This has an immediate positive effect. However, residential property owners will inevitably return to complaining both about rising property taxes and the higher costs charged by local businesses. That is because it does not address the problem of ever-increasing operating costs.

The assessor is caught between competing interests. On the one hand, there is the statutory requirement to appraise all properties at their market value, and on the other, the need to satisfy a governing board that is feeling the heat of taxpayer pressure. In my forty-plus years in the appraisal profession, there were very few years when property values decreased and that was during a severe economic crisis. So, the local assessor is faced with the prospect of increased property values in virtually every appraisal cycle. That scares taxpayers, who confront their commissioner. That commissioner, in turn, confronts the assessor who has few good options. He or she could keep values the same, which is against most states' laws, or follow those laws to the letter and possibly upset those people who control their budget.

Commissioners have to approve a budget each year in an environment of increasing property values and taxpayer frustration. The budget process usually begins in the spring with each department developing its budget which is compiled into the total county budget. The assessor prepares a budget request that includes everything needed to appraise properties during the next year. These department requests are then compared to the reality of what can be generated under limits in the law. Finally, before the total budget can be finalized, the commission has to decide how much of an increase the taxpaying public will allow. Their decision is a combination of sound management and political calculation. If they decide the public, they serve will not tolerate the increase proposed, they will order budget reductions.

The Public

It is very easy to get so caught up in what you are doing that you forget to think about how it might be interpreted by someone else. Couple this with poorly developed expectations and you have described nearly every first encounter I had with property owners as an appraiser/assessor. Both property owners and assessors believe the other party is going to mistreat them. So, they approach the meeting with their defenses up and ready to counter any blow by the opposition.

Now, I am a nice guy, at least I think I am. But I was told by some of my colleagues that I don't spend enough time explaining things. As a student, it meant I jumped right to the answer and spent little if any time explaining how I got there. As a teacher, that meant I didn't spend sufficient time explaining a concept to students. I was focused on the part of me that wanted not only to be right but to be the first one who was right. I had to learn that not everyone knows what I know or comprehends ideas in the same way or at the same speed – some faster, some slower. That required me to focus on the person I was talking to and to make sure they completely understood what I was talking about before I moved on. Still working on it.

The point is that every one of us shares our own set of character traits that set us apart and make us unique. The problem is they may also be misinterpreted by other people. My failure to completely explain a concept came across as uncaring. In meetings with property owners, it supported their preconceived notion that the government doesn't care about them and will run over them every chance it gets. I had to work very hard to overcome my bad habits, but in doing so, it made me appreciate and accept the fact that other people may have their problems.

For the general public, this generally meant a nervous introduction that manifested itself through timidity or anger. On the one hand, the person was so nervous they could not express their question or concern intelligently. It took a series of questions, asked as patiently as possible, to draw out the issue they wanted to present. On the other hand, it required waiting patiently as they vented their frustration at a "system" they thought was working against them. In both cases, their issue was with a heartless bureaucracy, not with the assessor. In neither case were they ready to hear an explanation. Only when the conversation moved beyond these points did it become productive for both parties.

In many cases, the assessor is the first step in the property tax process and often the only place where most property owners feel they can make a difference. This can be a stressful point for assessors and their staff, who work hard to make sure everything is accurate. I've had to remove staff from hearings and appeals when they couldn't separate their feelings and took a property owner's challenge to their assessment personally. It's tough to balance being proud of your work while also reviewing it fairly. Luckily, the majority of property owners just want their concerns addressed, and most assessors are ready to help.

How to Lose an Appeal

One event that guarantees tension between the assessor and the public is the first meeting that follows the mailing of value change notices. In the offices where I worked, these meetings were called informal hearings and they provided property owners an opportunity of ask questions about their value and offer evidence to reduce it. Unfortunately, many came in with little more than a statement that the value placed on their property was too high. Or, worse than that, they complained that their property taxes were too high. Either one of those arguments guaranteed the property owner lost their appeal.

Even in those states where the law has placed the burden of proof on the assessment office, assessment staff enter those meetings confident the values are correct. They will have, or certainly should have, plenty of documentation to support that value. So, the natural response to "my value is too high" is "No it isn't" and the response to "My taxes are too high" will be something like a sympathetic nod or "Mine are too high also".

I would ask property owners to keep in mind that the only reason to assess property is to distribute the tax burden. When values are fair that distribution is fair. When values are changed that distribution changes. When a value is lowered, that means the taxes formerly paid by one property are shifted to all other properties. The assessor is effectively defending all other property owners from that redistribution.

How to Win an Appeal

Winning an appeal and getting a value reduction, is actually quite simple with the right approach. First, prepare for the appeal by checking the data. By that I mean look over the records the assessor has on your property to check for possible errors. Every office I worked in would allow the property owner to have access to our parcel record on their property. This record, sometimes called a property record card, may look similar to one of the following images. Ask the assessor's office for a copy of that record and you may also need a description of each of the fields, to fully understand what has been recorded.

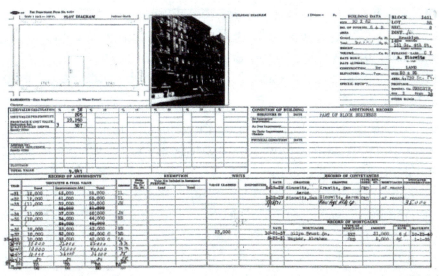

23 SAMPLE STREET, SAMPLE

Deed: SAMPLE JANE D	Map Area: Sample 1111 Res	Checks/Tags:
Contract:	Route: 000-000-000	Lister/Date: LF, 09/12/2011
CID#: 0000000000000	Tax Dist: Sample City-Test Comm	Review/Date: DS, 04/26/2012
DBA:	Plat Page: 000 - SE NE 00-00-7	Entry Status: Inspected
MLS:	Subdiv: CUMMINGS 1ST	

rban/Residential
egal: CUMMINGS 1ST

Land

Land Basis	Front	Rear	Side 1	Side 2	R. Lot	SF	Acres	Destrmnt	EFF/Type	Qual/Land	Unit Price	Total	Topo	Econ	Other	$Adj	LAND TYPE (Rnd Mkt Value)
cre X Rate						43,560.00	1.000			R-230	$70,000.00	570,000	0%	0%	0%	$0	$70,000
rand Total						43,560.00	1.000					$70,000					$70,000

Street	Utilities	Zoning	Land Use
cre X Rate Paved	City	Not Applicable	Not Applicable

Sales			Building Permits					Values			
Date	$ Amount	NUTC	Recording	Date	Number	Tag	$ Amount	Reason	Type	Appraised	B of R	St. Equalized	Pr Yr 2007
7/01/1997	$75,000	D034	3511/134						Land	$70,000	$0	$0	$49,546
									LandC		$0	$0	
									Dwlg	$779,700	$0	$0	$941,771
									Impr		$0	$0	
									Total	$849,700	$0	$0	$991,317

Res. Structure		Finish		Plumbing		Addition		Garage	
cc Code	101	To Rooms Above #	10 Bedrooms Above # 4	Full Bath	2	Addition	1 of 4	Garage	1 of 1
cc Decor	Single-Family / Owner Occupied	To Rooms Below #	5 Bedrooms Below # 0	Shower Stall Bath	1	Year Built	1997	Style	Att Frm
ter Built	1997	Lvng Qtrs (Mult)	2175 $25.50	Toilet Room	1	EFA	16	W X L	0' X 0'
FA / EFYr	16 / 1997			Lavatory	5	EFA Year	1997	Area (SF)	1,049
ch Dsgn	N/A	Foundation	Conc / C Blk	Water Closet		Style	1 Sty Frm	Year Built	1997
yle	2 Story Frame	Exterior Walls	Stn	Sink	2	Area (SF)	60	EFA	16
		Roof	Asph / Hip	Shower Stall/Tub		Condition	Normal	EFF Year	1997
		Interior Finish	Drwl	Mtl St Sh Bath		Pry-Depr %	19.00	Grade	Main Building
teaSF/TLA	1,884 / 6,969	Flooring	Hdwd	Mtl Stall Shower		Bsmt (SF)	60	Condition	NML
iLA 1st Dric	5,057 / 1,912			No Bathroom		NoBsmt Fn(SF)		Bsmt (SF)	
		Non-base Heating	Fireplace	Wet Bar	1	Heat	FHA - Gas	Qtrs Over	Frame
rade	E	Floor/Wall # 0	Prefab, 1 Sty 2	Whirlpool Bathroom		AC	Yes	Qtrs Over (SF)	178
		Pipeless # 0	Masonry-Double Side, 2 Sty	Whirlpool Tub		ABC (SF)		Qtrs AC (SF)	178
race Mult	2.330	Hand Fired (Y/N) No		No Hot Water Tank		See other pages for more additions		%Pry/Fcos/Ecos	19.00-15-0
ondition	NML	Space Heat # 0		No Plumbing				Door Opnrs	
ry-Depr %	19%	Appliances		Sewer & Water Only		Obsolescence		Stairs - Bsmt / Stc	
acement	Full	Range Unit Built-in Vacuums		Water Only w/Sink		Functional %	15%		
a Bsmt Fn		Oven - Single Intercom System		Hot Tub		Economic %	0%		
eat	FHA - Gas	Oven - Double Bl Stereo		Bidet		Other %	0%		
c	Yes	Dishwasher		Fbgls Service Sink		Architec/Design			
		Microwave		Urinal		Over-improved			
bc	None	Trash Compactor		Sauna		None			
		Jennair		W'Pool Bath w/Shower	1	None			
		Security System						© 1995-2015 Vanguard Appraisals, inc (rev 20.0.32.3276)	

Carefully review this record for any errors that can affect the value estimate. The year the property was built and the physical condition rating influence the amount of depreciation applied. The square footage of all living areas will also greatly impact the value, along with details like the basement area and the story height. (Keep in mind that assessors measure buildings from the outside walls to include the walls and foundation in cost estimates.)

Make a note of any differences so they can be pointed out during your hearing. Locate any written evidence you may have to support the differences, such as building construction plans and/or building and occupancy permits. Many jurisdictions have adopted a policy that prohibits assessment staff from entering any homes. Pictures of every room in the house may help support an argument on the number of rooms and bathrooms. If the assessor agrees with the changes you find, make sure the property record is changed to impact future valuations. Also, ask the assessor to recalculate the value based on those changes to determine if there is a change. Keep in mind, that some property characteristics are captured for reasons other than valuation.

Keep each of the three approaches discussed earlier in mind. Ask the assessor when you ask for the property record card, which of the three approaches was relied on to produce the final value.

Cost

If the cost approach was relied upon to produce the final value, the most important property characteristics to review are size, type of construction, quality of construction, physical condition and age. Size is represented by the square feet, or possibly cubic feet, for each floor of a building. In most cases, especially for residential property, this will be relatively easy to verify. Construction type is broadly divided into the classes of masonry and frame, with masonry being the more expensive. The specific rating used for construction quality will vary from one jurisdiction to another based on the underlying cost system. The property record card will probably contain only the rating of the subject property, so ask where that falls in the total rating scheme and, when in doubt, ask for a copy of that scheme. Physical condition is also represented as a rating and the same suggestions apply as the quality rating. Finally, age may or may not be recorded. Usually, it is a function of the year built. Make sure the recorded year built is the same as the actual, as it will be used in conjunction with other factors to establish the amount of depreciation to be applied.

Comparable Sales

When the final value is produced through the comparable sales approach, the important information is going to be on a comparable sales sheet like that shown below. This form is used to show the characteristics of the property being appraised along with those of three to five properties that sold before the date of the appraisal. The sample below uses the Uniform Residential Appraisal Report that is used by single property appraisers, but it contains many of the elements that will be found in most assessment offices.

Property characteristics are listed under the column headed FEATURE in our sample. In some cases, a code will be used to indicate the characteristic found on either the SUBJECT or one of the comparable sales. Be sure to ask the assessor for an explanation of any code or characteristic that is not clear to you.

Notice there are two columns under each comparable sale. Each property characteristic of the comparable that matches the item listed under the FEATURE column is shown under the column headed DESCRIPTION. For example, look for the line in the left-hand FEATURE column that says "Actual Age". Notice the number 11 under the SUBJECT column and the number 24 under the DESCRIPTION column for Comparable Sale #1. Notice the numbers 0 and 3 for comparable sales 2 and 3.

Recall the discussion of the three approaches to value earlier in this publication. Within the discussion of the comparable sales approach one of the key issues was the idea that the selling prices of the comparable sale properties had to be adjusted for differences between their characteristics and that of the property being appraised. When the characteristic was thought to decrease the value of the comparable property below that of the subject, the adjustment that was applied was positive to raise the value back up. When the characteristics were thought to increase the value of the comparable property above that of the subject, the adjustment that was applied was negative to adjust the sale price downward toward the subject.

This process is illustrated on the "Actual Age" line with each of the comparable sales. Comparable sale #1 shows a positive adjustment of 2,000 to account for the fact that it is 13 years older than the subject property. Because buildings tend to lose some of their value with age, this adjustment is acceptable in terms of its direction (positive versus negative). The appraiser thought the ages of comparable sales 2 and 3 were close to that of the subject and therefore, didn't need any adjustment.

Of course, age isn't the only factor affecting the rate a building deteriorates, construction quality and the level of maintenance reflected in the building's current condition are also indicators of that rate. In this case, all three comparable sales have been rated the same construction quality as the subject property and the adjustment columns show a zero for each property.

The condition rating tells a different and somewhat confusing story. The fact that a code is used highlights the need for the property owner to request clarification on both the meaning and the range of such codes. The condition rating used in the sample is taken from a rating schedule that ranges from a high of C1 to a low of C6. C1 is applied to new construction that has not been occupied at all or for only a short time. A rating of C2 reflects a building that is either new or major components have been replaced or completely renovated. There are no obvious signs of wear and tear in either rating. The

C3 rating reflects a well-maintained structure with limited depreciation due to wear and tear.

Comparable sale 1 has the same rating as the subject, so there is no adjustment required. Comparable sale 2, which had an age of 0, shows a negative adjustment of 10,000, because a new version of the subject property would tend to sell for a higher price than the subject. On the other hand, comparable sale 3 has a positive adjustment even though it has a condition rating higher than the subject. That doesn't make appraisal sense and a property owner can reasonably challenge that.

CHARACTERISTIC	SUBJECT	COMPARABLE #1	± Adjustment	COMPARABLE #2	± Adjustment	COMPARABLE #3	± Adjustment
Address	400 W Morse	502 E Grant		350 W Jackson		460 W Lee	
Sale Price		$300,000		$236,000		$235,000	
Sale Price/Gross Liv Area		$72		$102		$80	
VALUE ADJUSTMENTS	ITEM	ITEM	± Adjustment	ITEM	± Adjustment	ITEM	± Adjustment
Sale Date		3 months		2 months		3 months	
Site	15205 sf	32184 sf	-14,415	9800 sf	4,594	13200 sf	1,704
Style	Ranch	Ranch		Ranch		Ranch	
Quality of Construction	Average	Average		Average		Average	
Chronological Age	11	24	2,000	0		3	
Room Count	13/5/3.0	8/3/2.0	2,000	8/3/2.0	2,000	8/4/3.1	-1,000
Gross Living Area	2862 sf	4176 sf	-19,710	2310 sf	8,280	2995 sf	-1,395
Finished Basement Living Area	0	0		0		0	
Heating and Cooling	Central	Central		Central		Central	
Garage/Carport	2 Car Att	2 Car Att		None	4,000	2 Car Att	
Net Adjustment			-30,125		18,874		-691
Adjusted Sale Price			$269,875		$254,874		$234,309

In theory, a good appraiser can take any sale and adjust its selling price to reflect the subject property. In practice, the quality of an appraisal is measured by how similar the selected sale properties are to the subject. So, decide for yourself whether the assessor used the most comparable sales available. Remember, the assessor can only use what is *available* and the number of sales *available* for him or her to use may be very limited. Most states have laws requiring the disclosure of information held by government offices and you can take advantage of those to ask the local assessor for sale records maintained by that office. Keep in mind that the same laws that keep sales out of the hands of the assessor may also prohibit disclosure of that information by the assessment office. If you know of a sale that is more comparable than those used by the assessor, ask that it be considered as part of the appeal.

Finding an error on the property record is the easiest way for a property owner to win an appeal. An error on the subject property record will affect the entire comparable sales report. Property owners should ask the assessor for a copy of the comparable sales report and carefully review the property characteristics.

Another thing to look for is what is referred to as the "direction" of adjustments. The purpose of any adjustment is to make a comparable property's characteristics match those of the property being appraised. The sale price of a house that is not as nice as the property being appraised will have to be increased to make it match. That requires a positive (+) adjustment. The sale price of a house that is nicer than the property being appraised will have to be lowered. That requires a negative (-) adjustment. A direction error occurs when these signs are reversed because this will cause an error in the total adjusted value of the sale property.

Income

When the income approach is used to estimate the property value, there are three basic components to keep in mind: income, expenses, and capitalization rate. The income the assessor should use is the amount that would typically be generated from renting the subject building. Actual rent is useful, but it depends on the negotiating abilities of the parties involved rather than on just the building itself. A pattern will be revealed as more rental information is gathered. That pattern will show what the market considers typical for the type of building being appraised. The same is true for determining the typical expenses. The assessor must carefully analyze income and expense statements to determine which items are typical in the market. Additional analysis will establish the appropriate capitalization rate to be applied to the net income calculated from the market income and market expenses.

Assessors generally have a difficult time getting enough income and expense information. Owners and managers are hesitant to give that information to government employees. For that reason, it is rare for assessors to rely on the income approach. Instead, they may use it to support the value generated by one of the other two approaches. In theory, applying all three approaches to a single property should result in identical estimates of value. In practice, the amount and quality of information available to any one of those three approaches will vary enough to force a reliance on no more than two and sometimes only one of the three.

Be prepared to present actual income and expenses for the property being appealed and to explain to what extent and why those may differ from the typical.

The Future

I would like to get something out of the way at the top of this discussion. Assessors as a group tend not to be the first to implement new technology or approaches to their work and there are several reasons for that. First, as government employees, they are not highly paid relative to their counterparts in the private sector. Therefore, with some notable exceptions, the position tends to draw persons more interested in a steady paycheck than blazing new trails. Second, one of the ways county commissioners appease their constituents is by keeping budgets as low as possible, which does not translate into research and development. Finally, the technology in an assessment office is more often than not summed up in its CAMA system.

CAMA

CAMA stands for computer-assisted mass appraisal. It is most commonly thought of as a computer software package, but its influence extends far beyond the computer. Every system I have seen has its strengths and weaknesses and is comprised of basically three units: assessment administration, valuation, and reporting. Assessment administration keeps track of basic information regarding property ownership and tracks changes in that area. The valuation system supports the three approaches to value, with heavy emphasis on the cost approach and the reporting system provides output from the other two systems. Companies who market these systems know that they will have to modify the assessment administration and the reporting systems to accommodate the laws of the jurisdiction buying or licensing their system. However, they are hesitant to make changes within the valuation system and will not make any changes without being paid to do it (see "budgets as low as possible"). The market for CAMA systems is relatively small, which means there is very little incentive for any of the companies in that field to engage in research and development unless a specific client requests it and pays for it. Therefore, the assessor is faced with adapting to the CAMA system, especially in the area of valuation.

As an example, the very first CAMA system I worked with required the appraiser to measure the footprint of every house on the outside. This is common practice in appraisal and was expected. What was unexpected was that a formula was then used to calculate the upper floor areas of multi-story structures to calculate the total square footage of a home. This made for some interesting discussions with property owners who brought in construction plans that showed something different than what was calculated. To its credit, that CAMA vendor has since allowed for measurements of every floor individually. But this particular feature affected everything from initial data collection through final valuation and of course, value defense. That is what I meant when I said the CAMA system affects more than just entering data into a program.

One of the strengths of this vendor's product was the capability of calculating a new value from a prior year based on a change in one or more property characteristics. This is crucial since value appeals may extend over multiple years. The final decision may override that of the local assessor on something that affects value. This capability is made possible by "freezing" both the property record and key components of the valuation system for each tax year. In other words, at the time processing begins for a new tax year, the system stores a record of the previous year including the sales and income and expense files and the valuation models that were used with them. That allows those files and models to be retrieved and accurately recreate the values generated during that tax year. They can also be used to generate a new value from a change ordered on appeal as if the value had been generated at that time with the ordered change.

Artificial Intelligence

The previous discussion is important to provide a basis for my opinion that AI will not be entering the assessment world as a final value generator very soon. The ability to develop and freeze a valuation model is essential to assessors in today's legal and political climate. The AI models available to the public today don't advertise that capability.

The artificial intelligence systems I read about are based on artificial neural networks, These networks represent an attempt to match what happens in the human brain. Their components are even referred to as neurons. An artificial neural network is comprised of three layers: an input layer, a hidden layer, where transformations and processing of data take place, and an output layer. The user controls what data enters the input layer and receives the output. There is, however, no model for the user to tweak and change how the input is transformed into the output, which may change the next time the program is run.

For example, I asked an AI system for the market value of my property and at one point received the answer that it is "between $229,000 and $273,000". When I asked it again, it came back with $237,071, which to my mind is not a bad estimate. However, this time it also included a range between $209,509 and $270,756.

This would never work in a local assessment office. The assessor has to be able to rely on the valuation model producing the same value every time the model is run until either the inputs or the model structure changes. That is why the data used as input and the models themselves are copied and saved after each tax year. That procedure provides both the assessor and property owners with the security that the value on which taxes were based can be replicated. It also provides appeal bodies with the assurance that they can rely on the accuracy of a new value that is generated using the old data and model when they order a change in the property characteristics.

On the other hand, artificial intelligence tools may be very useful in the analysis of the real estate market. The ability to discover and track trends is essential to the development of models in all three approaches to value and AI may prove to be very helpful in that regard.

Legislation

One area that is bound to change is the set of laws that govern assessors. Legislators come and go but they are all sympathetic with the complaints of their constituents. This invariably leads to tinkering with the property tax system. They tinker instead of making massive changes because, even with their lack of knowledge of how the system works, they quickly learn that massive changes to the property tax system translate into equally massive and possibly costly disruptions. Those disruptions, in turn, may cause their constituents to lose the services they want to keep. The typical result is a shift in the property tax burden coupled with additional work for the assessor to track a new exemption or classification. Of course, there is no additional money to pay for extra staff since the objective of the "tinker" was to save tax dollars. So, everyone from the assessor through to the treasurer must perform extra work with already strained resources.

Not Much Changes

Not much changed during the 40+ years I spent in the assessment profession. Each year assessors performed the duties their predecessors did. Except for legislation, change comes slowly to assessment offices, which is good for both the assessors and the public they serve. The job of maintaining an accurate assessment roll year after year is difficult enough without adding the challenges of adapting to changes imposed from the outside and explaining them to property owners. The assessor is on the front lines of the property tax system and therefore bears the brunt of any criticism, even when the issue being criticized is beyond the reach of the assessor. That also won't change and good assessors, like good policemen and firemen and bankers and stock brokers, will continue doing their job as best they can.

Glossary of Terms

A

Adjustment
A modification made to the selling price of a comparable property to account for differences between it and the subject property, such as size, age, or features.

Adjustment Direction
The sign (positive or negative) of an adjustment made during the sales comparison approach to align a comparable property's characteristics with the subject property. A positive adjustment increases the value, and a negative adjustment decreases it.

Appeal Process
A formal procedure allowing property owners to contest the appraised value of their property. The burden of proof may rest with the property owner or the assessor, depending on jurisdiction.

Appraisal
An estimate of value, typically market value or fair market value, which represents the price a willing buyer would pay to a willing seller in an open market without undue pressure or incomplete information.

Appraisal Cycle
The recurring period during which properties are reassessed to reflect changes in market value, typically resulting in adjustments to property taxes.

Appraisal Level
The overall accuracy of appraisals, measured by comparing the appraised value of properties to their actual selling prices using statistical methods like the median ratio.

Appraised Value
The value assigned to a property by the assessor, used as the numerator in ratio studies to evaluate appraisal accuracy.

Appraiser

A professional who estimates the value of property. In the context of assessors, appraisers focus on values for tax purposes, whereas private appraisers often work for real estate transactions or lending purposes.

Approaches to Value

The three primary methods appraisers use to estimate the value of property: **cost approach**, **comparable sales approach**, and **income approach**. Each method is applied based on the property type and available market data.

Assessment Equity

The principle that all properties within a jurisdiction should be appraised at their market value to ensure a fair distribution of the property tax burden.

Assessment Roll

A record of all properties in a jurisdiction, including their appraised values, used to determine property taxes.

Assessor

A type of appraiser who evaluates the value of real and personal property for property tax purposes. The role is governed by legislative directives and often involves mass appraisal techniques.

B

Base Cost

The initial cost of construction before adding any specialized features or amenities such as heating, cooling, or additional space.

Board of County Commissioners

The governing body of a county, responsible for approving budgets, setting policies, and addressing taxpayer concerns, including those related to property taxes.

Budget Process

The annual procedure where county departments, including the assessor's office, submit funding requests, which are reviewed and adjusted to align with revenue projections and taxpayer tolerance for increases.

C

Capitalization Rate (Cap Rate)
A percentage that reflects the relationship between a property's net operating income (NOI) and its value. It is calculated as NOI divided by the property's sale price and is used to estimate property value in the income approach.

Classification
The practice of categorizing property types (e.g., residential, commercial, industrial) and applying different assessment rates, which can shift the tax burden between property classes.

Coefficient of Dispersion (COD)
Expresses as a percentage the average deviation of the ratios from the median. The COD is used throughout the property assessment field as a measure of appraisal uniformity. (International Association of Assessing Officers. (2021).)

Commercial Properties
Buildings used for business purposes, such as retail stores or office buildings, that are often valued based on their income-generating potential.

Common Data
Shared data collected and maintained by mass appraisers, including property characteristics and market information, to ensure consistency and efficiency in valuation.

Comparable Sale
A property that has recently sold and shares similar characteristics with the subject property, used as a basis for valuation in the sales comparison approach.

Comparable Sales Approach
See **Sales Comparison Approach**

Comparable Sales Report
A document detailing the sales of properties used as comparables in the appraisal process, showing their characteristics, adjustments, and adjusted sale prices.

Computer Assisted Mass Appraisal (CAMA)
A software system used by assessors to calculate property values, often incorporating cost tables and other data for efficiency.

Condition Rating
A classification that reflects a building's physical state, maintenance, and wear, often coded (e.g., C1–C6) to represent varying levels of condition.

Consistency
A key principle in mass appraisal ensuring that all appraisers rate and value properties in the same manner using standardized methods.

Contributory Value
The value added to a property by a specific feature or component, determined through methods such as paired sales analysis.

Cost Approach
1) One of the three approaches to value, the cost approach is based on the principle of substitution—that a rational, informed purchaser would pay no more for a property than the cost of building an acceptable substitute with like utility. The cost approach seeks to determine the replacement cost new of an improvement less depreciation plus land value; and 2) The method of estimating the value of property by: (a) Estimating the cost of construction based on replacement or reproduction cost new or trended historical cost (often adjusted by a local multiplier); (b) Subtracting depreciation; and (c) Adding the estimated land value. (The land

value is most frequently determined by the sales comparison approach.) (International Association of Assessing Officers. (2021))

Cost Approach Formula
A mathematical representation of the cost approach:
$(RCN-DEP)+LAND=COST(RCN - DEP) + LAND = COST$
Where RCN = Replacement cost new, DEP = Depreciation, and LAND = Land value.

Cost Manual
A standardized guide, often nationally recognized, that provides cost tables for estimating building replacement costs. Adjustments are made for local conditions and market changes.

D

Depreciation
A reduction in the value of a building over time due to factors such as wear and tear, changes in market preferences, or external economic factors.

- **Physical Depreciation**: Loss of value due to natural wear and tear or age of the structure.

- **Functional Obsolescence**: Loss of value caused by outdated features or design that reduce the building's utility or desirability.

- **Economic Obsolescence**: Loss of value due to external factors, such as undesirable developments near the property.

E

Effective Age
An adjusted age of a property reflecting its condition and any improvements, rather than its actual chronological age.

Economic Life
The estimated period during which a building remains useful and

retains its value, typically measured as 60 years for wood frame houses.

Equity
The principle that all properties within a jurisdiction should be appraised fairly and consistently, ensuring a proportional tax burden.

F

Fair Market Value
The price a property would sell for in a competitive and open market under typical conditions for the market.

Functional Obsolescence
A decrease in property value due to outdated or inefficient design elements, such as poor bathroom placement or lack of modern heating/cooling systems.

G

Goodwill
An intangible asset representing the value of a business beyond its physical assets and inventory, often considered in commercial property sales.

Governing Board
An elected or appointed body that oversees local government operations, including budget approval and addressing property tax concerns.

Gross Living Area (GLA)
The total square footage of finished, above-grade residential space, used to calculate value in appraisals.

H

Highest and Best Use
The most profitable and feasible use of a property, which is legal, physically possible, and maximizes return to a prospective buyer.

Determining this use is critical in areas experiencing changes in property usage.

I

Income Approach
One of the three approaches to value that converts expected economic benefits of owning a property into value through a direct capitalization method or yield capitalization process. Also called Income Capitalization Approach. (International Association of Assessing Officers. (2021))

Income Approach Formula
A mathematical representation of the income approach:
$V=I/R$V = I / R
Where VV = Property value, II = Net operating income, and RR = Capitalization rate.

Inequity
A situation where inconsistent appraisals lead to an unfair distribution of the property tax burden among property owners.

Informal Hearing
An initial meeting where property owners can discuss their appraisal concerns with the assessor and present evidence to support a value adjustment.

L

Legislative Advocacy
The process by which assessors and professional associations lobby for changes to property tax laws to improve appraisal practices or ensure taxpayer fairness.

Location Adjustment
An adjustment made to costs in a manual to reflect differences in construction expenses, labor rates, or transportation costs in different geographical areas.

Lump Sum Adjustment
A single dollar amount added to or subtracted from a comparable property's selling price for specific features, such as the presence of a fireplace.

M

Management Fee
An expense associated with the operation of a commercial property, representing payment for property management services. Typical management fees are included in operating expenses for appraisal purposes.

Market Data
Information about property sales, including prices and characteristics, used to support appraisals and valuation models.

Market Modeling
The use of statistical tools, such as regression analysis, to identify patterns and relationships in sales data, aiding in property valuation.

Market Rental Rates
The typical income a property can generate from rent under standard market conditions, as determined by assessing comparable properties.

Market Value
A value, stated as an opinion, that presumes the transfer of a property (i.e., a right of ownership or a bundle of such rights), as of a certain date, under specific conditions set forth in the value definition that is identified by the appraiser as applicable in an appraisal. (International Association of Assessing Officers. (2021))

Mass Appraisal
A systematic method of appraising a large number of properties simultaneously using common data, standardized methods, and statistical testing.

Mathematical Models
Formulas representing relationships within the real estate market, used in the cost, sales comparison, and income approaches to estimate property values.

Median Ratio
The middle value of a ranked set of appraisal ratios, representing the central tendency of the data. It is not influenced by outliers and is used to assess the level of appraisal accuracy.

Mean
The average of all appraisal ratios in a dataset, calculated by summing the ratios and dividing by the number of ratios. Unlike the median, the mean is affected by outliers.

Mis-Improvement
A structure or use that is inconsistent with the highest and best use of the land, such as a residential property on a commercial plot, potentially reducing the value of the improvement.

Multiple Regression Analysis
A statistical method used to examine relationships among multiple property characteristics and their impact on sales prices, often employed in mass appraisal.

N

Negative Adjustment
A decrease in the comparable property's sale price during appraisal to account for superior characteristics relative to the subject property.

Net Operating Income (NOI)
The income a property generates from rent after subtracting typical operating expenses but excluding owner-specific costs like mortgage payments or business profits.

Noise
Unpredictable variations in the real estate market, such as

differences in buyer preferences or negotiating skills, which cannot be measured or standardized by appraisers.

O

Operating Expenses
The costs necessary for the day-to-day operation of a property, such as maintenance, utilities, and management fees. Non-operational costs, like mortgage payments, are excluded from this category for appraisal purposes.

Outliers
Unusually high or low values in a dataset that deviate significantly from other observations, potentially distorting statistical measures like the mean.

Oversight Agency
A state-level organization ensuring that local assessors meet legal and professional standards for property valuation and taxation.

P

Paired Sales Analysis
A technique for determining the value of a specific property feature by comparing two nearly identical sales, differing only in the presence or absence of that feature.

Parcel Record/Property Record Card
A detailed record of a property's physical and legal characteristics maintained by the assessor's office, often used in appeals to verify accuracy.

Percent Good
The remaining value of a property as a percentage of its replacement cost new, after accounting for depreciation.

Personal Property
Movable property not attached to the land or buildings, such as cars, furniture, clothing, and jewelry.

Physical Condition Rating

A rating used to capture the physical state of a property, factoring in wear and tear and maintenance levels.

Positive Adjustment

An increase in the comparable property's sale price during appraisal to account for inferior characteristics relative to the subject property.

Price Related Differential (PRD)

A statistical measure of vertical property tax equity. The PRD is calculated by dividing the mean ratio by the weighted mean ratio in a ratio study. If the result exceeds 1.03, assessments are considered regressive. If the result is less than 0.98, assessments are considered progressive. (International Association of Assessing Officers. (2021))

Property Tax System

A system based on market value appraisals to distribute the property tax burden equitably among property owners. A framework through which local governments generate revenue by taxing property owners based on the appraised value of their properties.

Q

Quality of Construction

An attribute of a property referring to the materials and craftsmanship used in its construction, influencing its market value.(see Quality Rating)

Quality Rating

A rating that reflects the materials, construction quality, and design complexity of a building. A classification in cost tables that reflects the quality of construction materials and craftsmanship of a building.

R

Ratio
A comparison of a property's appraised value to its actual selling price, used in ratio studies to evaluate appraisal accuracy and consistency. Formula: **Appraised Value / Selling Price**.

Ratio Study
A statistical analysis used in mass appraisal to measure appraisal performance by comparing appraised values to actual selling prices using key metrics: the median, COD, and PRD.

Ratio Study Standards
Statistical standards used to evaluate the accuracy and equity of property assessments within a jurisdiction.

Real Property
Land and anything permanently attached to it, such as buildings, as well as the associated rights of ownership.

Replacement Cost New (RCN)
The cost to construct a building with the same utility as the original, using modern materials and techniques.

Reproduction Cost
The cost to construct an exact replica of a building, replicating the original materials and techniques.

Residential Property
Homes and other dwellings, often representing the largest portion of the tax base, and frequently the focus of taxpayer complaints about high property taxes.

Return of Investment
The recovery of the original amount invested in a property, typically achieved through a combination of income and resale value.

Return on Investment
The profit earned on a property, measured as income generated during ownership or from its eventual resale.

S

Sales Analysis
A method for estimating depreciation by analyzing recent property sales, subtracting land value, and comparing with replacement costs.

Sales Comparison Approach
One of three approaches to value, the sales comparison approach estimates a property's value (or some other characteristic, such as depreciation) by reference to comparable sales. The sales comparison approach compares recently sold properties to the subject property. Adjustments are made to comparable properties to reflect the characteristics of the subject property. (International Association of Assessing Officers. (2021))

Sales Comparison Approach Formula
A mathematical representation of the sales comparison approach:
$Vs = Sc \pm Adjc$ $Vs = Sc \pm Adjc$
Where Vs Vs = Subject property value, Sc Sc = Sale price of comparable property, and $Adjc$ $Adjc$ = Adjustments.

Selling Price
The actual transaction price of a property, used as the denominator in ratio studies. The price at which a property is sold. In the income approach, it is used along with NOI to calculate the capitalization rate.

Single Property Appraiser
An appraiser who evaluates individual properties one at a time, often for purposes such as real estate transactions or bank loans.

Standardized Methods
Established procedures and guidelines used by mass appraisers to ensure uniformity and reliability in property valuations.

Statistical Testing
The use of statistical methods to analyze trends, verify consistency,

and ensure accuracy in mass appraisal processes. The application of statistical tools, such as the median ratio, COD, and PRD, to evaluate the accuracy and fairness of appraisals in mass appraisal systems.

Statutory Disclosure
A legal requirement for property sales information to be disclosed to appraisal officials, aiding in accurate property valuation.

Subject Property
The property being appraised, whose value is being estimated using comparable sales or other appraisal approaches.

T

Tax Burden Shift
The redistribution of property taxes from one class of property (e.g., residential) to another (e.g., commercial), often as a result of changes in assessment practices or classification rates.

Taxpayer Pressure
The influence exerted by property owners on elected officials to lower taxes or challenge increases, often in response to rising property values.

Total Depreciation
The cumulative reduction in a property's value due to physical deterioration, functional obsolescence, and economic obsolescence.

Transparency in Appraisal
Efforts by assessors and legislators to make the property valuation process clearer and more accessible, ensuring that property owners understand how values are determined and taxes are calculated.

Typical Management
The standard practices of managing a property, including setting

rents, maintaining facilities, and collecting payments, which are considered when assessing market conditions.

U

Uniform Residential Appraisal Report (URAR)
A standardized form used in residential property appraisals, documenting property characteristics, comparable sales, and adjustments.

Utility
The usefulness or functional value of a building to its owner or tenant.

V

Vacant Land
Land without structures, which must be appraised using methods other than the cost approach.

Value Change Notice
A formal notice sent to property owners when their appraised property value changes, typically triggering the option to appeal.

Valuation Model
A mathematical or computational framework used in mass appraisal to estimate property values based on collected data and defined variables.

Valuation Appeal
A challenge to an assessed property value, often involving disputes over methods, data, or assumptions used in the appraisal process.

Variables
Factors that influence the value of a property, such as size, quality, location, and market trends.

W

Weighted Mean
A type of mean that accounts for the total appraised values and

selling prices, offering a more balanced measure when calculating the PRD. Formula: **Total Appraised Value / Total Selling Price**.

References

International Association of Assessing Officers. (2021). "IAAO Glossary of Property Appraisal and Assessment". Retrieved from [IAAO website] (https://www.iaao.org/wp-content/uploads/IAAO-Glossary_3rd-Ed_final.pdf)

www.ingramcontent.com/pod-product-compliance
Lightning Source LLC
LaVergne TN
LVHW012337060326
832902LV00012B/1909